"What's the recipe for a happy family? While every family is unique, *Big Hearted* offers some of the 'secret ingredients' to creating a home that is happy, holy, and blessed. The authors blend their stories with personal accounts from other gifted writers to give insight into creating a home filled with love. Read this book and you'll be inspired to look at what being 'big hearted' looks like under your own roof and beyond."

—*Lisa M. Hendey, founder of* CatholicMom.com *and author of* A Book of Saints for Catholic Moms

"Despite being almost constantly surrounded by lots of people, raising a large family is often a lonely endeavor. Parents often find themselves essentially alone on the sidelines of neighborhood ballgames, at local school events, and even in the pews of typical parishes. This book is a like a glorious block party with warm, wise families who are all earnestly endeavoring to live a life of joy and grace. You will come away with a bigger heart for having read it."

—*Elizabeth Foss, co-author of* Small Steps for Catholic Moms

"*Big Hearted* is a true gift to the world! The stories of real families sharing their struggles and triumphs will inspire parents, grandparents and anyone looking to bring the blessing of children into their lives. *Big Hearted* is countercultural, and that is a very good thing. In a time of broken marriages, dysfunctional families, and a growing disregard for human life, this book has the courage to share numerous examples of what love and faith in God can achieve in creating wonderful families. Be prepared—this book is likely to have a profound effect on you and will leave a mark!"

—*Randy Hain, co-founder and senior editor of* Integrated Catholic Life *and author of* Something More: The P   ;ful Life

"*Big Hearted* is a one-of-a kind inspirational book, aimed straight at the heart of Christian families everywhere. This treasure trove of heartfelt stories will make you smile and cry and then hug your family all the tighter. Highly recommended."

—*Donna-Marie Cooper O'Boyle, author and EWTN TV host of* Everyday Blessings for Catholic Moms *and* Catholic Mom's Café

"Pope Paul VI once observed that modern men and women listen more willingly to witnesses than to teachers, and perhaps this is nowhere more true than in family life. *Big Hearted* presents a cloud of witnesses whose families are living proof that God is never outdone in generosity. If you are ready to have your heart stretched by stories of real families who struggle to love and to serve the people God has placed on their path, this book is for you."

—*Lisa Everett, co-director, Office of Family Life, Diocese of Fort Wayne–South Bend, Indiana*

"I couldn't put it down! Lovely stories and such a great variety! In a world where small families are the norm, having a large family seems wildly impractical. *Big Hearted* offers a glimpse into the lives of large families of all sorts: blended, biological, foster, adoptive, and inter-generational. These families may lack designer clothing, but they are blessed with a superabundance of people to love."

—*Leticia Velasquez, blogger at Cause of Our Joy and author of* A Special Mother Is Born

"The family is the place where the gospel is taught, observed, and shared—from generation to generation. In *Big Hearted*, you will be inspired by the faithfulness of everyday families. The possibility of your family walking in victory will come into an energizing focus."

—*Jeff Cavins, award-winning author, internationally renowned speaker, and creator of* The Great Adventure Catholic Bible Study

"As the founder of an apostolate dedicated to the cultivation of vocations to the priesthood, I believe there is only one area that's more important than fostering priestly vocations: marriage, family, and life issues. If we don't get those those things right, then our work of encouraging young men to consider the priesthood will be that much more difficult. In this book, Patti Armstrong, Teresa Thomas, and their collaborators have captured the spirit of what it means to be big hearted. And not a moment too soon. As the family goes, so goes our culture. And so goes the Church."

—*Jerry J. Usher, president, Third Millennium Media, LLC*

"Families are the cornerstone of society, yet due to overwhelming cultural pressures, our families are eroding more each decade. What can be done? In their empowering book, *Big Hearted: Inspiring Stories from Everyday Families,* Patti Armstrong and Theresa Thomas, show that with open hearts and God's grace, our families won't just survive, but will thrive! This collection of uplifting stories will touch your soul and inspire you to pick up three more copies to share with your friends—it's that good!"

—*Tom Peterson, founder of Virtue Media, Inc.*
and author of Catholics Come Home

"For me, my family has been both the source of my deepest wounds and the most profound healing and moments of grace in my life. The stories in this book have been a joyous reminder of God's ability to make all things new. If walls could talk in the homes where Christ is present and prominent, they would tell the story of human tragedy and triumph, of suffering and healing. Herein you will find a few of these beautiful stories of love and redemption where God, in spite of our human frailties, is alive and well in the hearts and around the hearths of homes where he is central."

—*Dan Burke, executive director of EWTN's* National Catholic Register *and author of the award-winning* Navigating the Interior Life

"Love, joy, laughs, tears, faith, doubts, sacrifices, and rewards are all part of the beautiful tapestry that make up a family. In *Big Hearted* Patti Armstrong, Theresa Thomas, and their contributors walk readers through their own experiences as parents, opening our minds and hearts to all the unexpected graces that family life has to offer. They'll help you better appreciate your own kids—or open yourself to the possibility of welcoming new life into your home."

—*Tony Rossi, director of communications, The Christophers*

"At a time when families are being undermined and devalued in our society, here is a book that celebrates and supports families. It is reassuring as well as instructive, since families don't come with instruction manuals. One of the values of strong families is their innate ability to impart wisdom and love to the next generation. Even if your own childhood was lacking or you are struggling to impart an example of unconditional love, these stories of love and overcoming hardships in the bond that is family provide a powerful example."

—*Teresa Tomeo, author, speaker, and syndicated Catholic radio talk-show host*

"Family life becomes a school of love when families discover the grace of unconditional love. The parents of *Big Hearted* share with us how entrusting the family to God's care bears fruit in ordinary and extraordinary ways."

—*Reverend Richard Kramer, associate director for Evangelization and Family Life, Archdiocese of Washington*

BIG
HEARTED

INSPIRING STORIES FROM EVERYDAY FAMILIES

Patti Armstrong & Theresa Thomas

Published by Scepter Publishers, Inc.
P.O. Box 1391
New Rochelle, NY 10802
www.scepterpublishers.org

Cover image: Shutterstock.com
Cover design and interior layout by Creative Editorial Solutions

ISBN: 978-1-59417-190-1

Printed in the United States of America

15 14 13 12   1 2 3 4

Whoever sows sparingly will also reap sparingly, and whoever sows bountifully will also reap bountifully. Each must do as already determined, without sadness or compulsion, for God loves a cheerful giver. Moreover, God is able to make every grace abundant for you, so that in all things, always having all you need, you may have an abundance for every good work... You are being enriched in every way for all generosity...

2 CORINTHIANS 9:6–11

DEDICATION

To my beloved family who has taught me that even when family life takes work, it is always worth it.

To my parents who showed me the meaning of both love and work.

To my husband, Mark, who has brought love and adventure into my life and saw the value of being open to life from the beginning. Thanks for your steadfast presence; I cannot imagine life without you.

To my children: Aaron, Luke, Tyler, Calvin, Jacob, Joash, Mary, Teresa, John, and Isaac. Each of you has expanded my heart and blessed me beyond measure. I am so grateful to God for each one of you.

ACKNOWLEDGMENTS

Thank you to all who have generously shared their heartwarming stories. Special thanks to John Powers who had the idea for this book and trusted us to write it. To the ever cheerful Nathan Davis, who hammered out the details, and to Claudia Volkman, who made everything look just right.

To my co-author Theresa Thomas, for your creativity, inspiration and friendship. What an honor it has been work with such a friend like you.

Thanks be to God for choosing me for such a project and giving me the life to go with it.

And finally, thank you dear reader, for picking up this book. My co-author and I will be praying for you, for writing the book is only the beginning.

—*Patti Maguire Armstrong*

DEDICATION

To my parents, Bonnie and Irvin Kloska, who first demonstrated to me the love and blessings that come from being big hearted.

To my amazing children David, Michael, Caroline, Matthew, Melissa, Rachel, Grace, Theresa, and Angela. I'm so proud of and love you all! There is no greater honor than to be your dad's wife and your mother.

To my "big hearted" siblings and their spouses and children, who make extended family interesting, fun and full of joy.

Most especially, to the strong and generous leader of our family, my husband David. I cannot imagine embarking on this grand adventure of love and life with anyone else but you. Thank you for providing and protecting, and for laying down your life for us. I'm hoping for fifty more years...at least. Love you!

ACKNOWLEDGMENTS

A heartfelt thank-you to my co-author Patti Armstrong. It's been wonderful working with someone so energetic and talented. Thank you to John Powers and Nathan Davis at Scepter, who brought the idea of this book to us, and to the encouraging and warm Claudia Volkman for her magic touch—wonderful editing, typesetting, and her integral part in selecting a beautiful cover for *Big Hearted*. Thank you to Tim Johnson, Randy Hain, and Deacon Mike Bickerstaff for the continued support of my work and providing a regular venue for my columns and ideas. Thank you to Elizabeth Foss, Leticia Velasquez, and Lisa Everett, amazing fellow moms who encourage me in many ways they may not even know. Thank you to our amazing contributors who opened their hearts to share their stories for the benefit of others.

Thank you, God. It is truly a wonderful life!

—*Theresa Kloska Thomas*

TABLE OF CONTENTS

INTRODUCTION

The child is God's gift to the family.
BLESSED MOTHER TERESA

The history of mankind, the history of salvation,
passes by way of the family...
POPE JOHN PAUL II

WHEN MOST BRIDES and grooms stand before the altar and say, "I do," little do they know the challenges that await them. While they dream about stepping over the threshold of their new home together, of babies and successful careers, they are mostly unaware of the reality around the corner. Settling into a new home may not happen for years; they may suffer miscarriages or face disability or disease. There may be the stress of the bills, to add to the challenge of loving daily.

"Ah, the naiveté of youth," the older people cluck as the newlyweds drive off blissfully in a sedan with the words "Just Married" scribbled in washable paint. "Just wait," some think. And presently, it's true, the couple will encounter what others before them have— the tests and the trials of daily married and family life.

What these young hopefuls also may not know, however,

is that just around the corner is more satisfaction and joy than they could have ever imagined. They will soon discover the blessings that come from enduring hardship together, along with surprising moments of delight when they open themselves to God's will. This is his gift to their generous "yes."

When a family opens its collective heart to love one another fully, there is no end to the gifts that God will bestow. It has been said that God cannot be outdone in generosity, and the stories in the following pages will show you how true this is.

Both my co-author and I have university degrees, years of work experience, and nineteen children between us. We are women with hopes and dreams, and none so big as those we have for our families.

In this book lies the heart of our desires. More than good students, athletes, and success at jobs, we want big-hearted families. No amount of studying or training can accomplish this for our children. Our big-hearted goal isn't opportunities or financial success; it's love. Love is something to which we all have access. It is a gift we can spend freely and end up with more than when we began.

The families in this book are just like ours, and probably just like yours, too. The similarity is not necessarily the outer details—every family is unique; it's the goal of striving to put God first, of trying to love well.

We are sometimes weak and imperfect, but love never fails. Love heals and overcomes adversity. It gives us strength and courage beyond our imagination. The source of this never-ending love is our faith in God. As the lives of the families who have generously shared their stories demonstrate, all of us struggle to impart God's love through our own humble efforts. This desire pulls us out of bad days and difficult circumstances and gives us the ability to overcome everything with love.

In this book, you will learn of family struggles with cancer, adoption, alcoholism, miscarriages, financial hardships, and disabilities—and you will read about family joy in these very situations. You will be invited to see extraordinary love in ordinary moments: the simple cooking of a meal or the hug between a teenaged brother and his baby sister. Just like your family, these families experience pain and challenges. And just like your family, they also experience love and immeasurable blessings. It is in the love of God and love of family that joy and healing triumph.

Beyond the stories included here, we invite you to look around and discover the miracles and blessings around you in your neighborhood, your parish, and your community. They are there in abundance. And don't forget to look inside the walls of your own home, where God's great mystery and love is revealed daily to those who are openhearted.

Sacrifice much. Choose God's will. Love profusely. Be big-hearted. And then see how our almighty God, who is the same now as always, blesses you again and again.

—*Patti Armstrong and Theresa Thomas*

THE KENYA CONNECTION

Patti Maguire Armstrong

WHY WOULD A family with eight kids already accept two teenage boys from Kenya—sight unseen?

It began when our friend Evan came to our home for dinner. He was in town for a mid-service break from his work as an English teacher in Kisii, Kenya—mission work sponsored by our Bismarck, North Dakota diocese. "Is there anything you need?" my husband Mark and I wanted to know.

A sly grin crossed Evan's face. "As a matter of fact, there is," he began. "I have a bright young student who desperately wants to go to school in the United States. Would you consider taking him in?"

Mark and I looked at one another.

"We can't," we said. We could barely afford the ones we had. We already had eight children, from a one-year-old to a nineteen-year-old in college: six boys and two girls.

"Yes," he said, nodding his head. "I knew that, so I wasn't going to ask you, but your name kept coming up when I asked others. Someone said, 'Have you asked the Armstrongs? They have so many they won't notice one more.'"

Then Evan brightened. "What if I got a family or two to help with the expenses?" He went on to tell us about Calvin. "He is a good boy. His parents died of AIDS, and he had been living with his two brothers. I found out he often went hungry and walked a long way to school." Evan had our attention. "I invited him to stay at the school with me during the week so he can eat properly. He wanted me to bring him back to the U.S., but I am almost seventy so that would be impossible."

At that point, it seemed unlikely that Calvin would actually get permission to leave the country. He was fifteen, had no birth certificate, and needed a passport and visa. We would have to become his legal guardians, and our medical insurance would need to cover him. Then, it would be necessary for St. Mary's High School, where our teenagers attended, to accept him on scholarship. There were so many hoops to jump through that it all seemed unlikely.

"We'll pray about it," we told Evan. "If it's God's will, it will happen." We never actually said yes. Our thinking was that we would take it one step at a time. A single insurmountable hurdle would shut it all down.

Before Evan left Bismarck, he found two families willing to help with Calvin's financial support. Six weeks later, Evan emailed us that Calvin had gotten a birth certificate. The wheels were in motion, and one by one, every hurdle was overcome.

In July 2002 Evan sent us an email. "Calvin just got his visa. He'll be there in two weeks." Not until that moment did it fully hit me. I was going to become the mother of a teenage boy from

Kenya. "Dear God," I prayed, "help us adjust." I also asked the Blessed Mother to pray for me and help me to be a good mother to Calvin.

On the day of Calvin's arrival, Mark was on a business trip with our high-school kids, so I went to the airport with the younger ones. I greeted Calvin as he got off the plane; mom and son—total strangers. He smiled nervously. I loaded everyone into our van and began driving. As I looked in the rearview mirror and saw Calvin talking with the younger children, a wave of peace washed over me. Everything was going to be okay.

When Mark returned with the older kids, Tyler, the same age as Calvin, was thrilled that his long-awaited "brother from the other color mother" had finally arrived. Luke, our seventeen-year-old, had persistently warned us that taking in another child would be too chaotic. Before he went to bed on Calvin's first night, he told me, "I'm glad he's here."

I thought we were just trying to be good Christians and help someone in need, but when I learned the rest of the story, I realized that we were the ones who had been blessed. God had chosen us to answer a prayer that bordered on the miraculous.

Years earlier, Calvin gently closed his paperback novel as he lay in his mud hut. It was getting dark in the two-room home he shared with his two brothers. There was no money for oil to burn in their kerosene lantern, so reading stopped at sunset. Ignoring the rumbling of his empty stomach, Calvin thought about the main character in his novel: a boy who left Africa to live with relatives in the United States and go to school there. "Maybe I could go there someday," Calvin dreamed.

"Dear God," he prayed, "Please let me go to school in the United States one day." Calvin prayed with the trust of a child, even though at thirteen, his childhood had been lost long ago. Both his parents had died of AIDS, leaving Rogers, fifteen; Calvin, eleven; and Joash, nine—just three of Kenya's 650,000 AIDS orphans. The boys had loved their parents deeply. The ache caused by their absence overshadowed each day.

Relatives helped out a little, but as time went on, the assistance was gradually withdrawn. An uncle continued to pay the fees for Calvin to attend school, but it was a long walk from his hut to St. Patrick's Elementary School. Since he rarely had dinner the night before, his feet felt heavy as he trudged along. "If only I could go to school in the United States," Calvin often thought on these long walks. And again, he prayed.

When Calvin revealed his prayer to his older brother and an aunt, they laughed. "You only own two pairs of pants and have no money," his aunt said. "How do you think you are going to get to the United States?"

"Why don't you pray for something more practical, like more land?" Rogers said. The boys' only source of food was a small garden and occasional donations of food from others.

Then, Evan Beauchamp came to work at St. Patrick's as a missionary teacher. When he noticed that Calvin had a sore on his foot that was not healing after several weeks, he knew it must be the effects of malnutrition. He invited Calvin to live with him during the week and then return home to help his brothers on weekends. Calvin overflowed with appreciation. It was not long before Calvin asked if Evan could take him back to the United States with him. Evan said that would never be possible. Calvin kept praying, and he kept asking. Finally, Evan told Calvin he would ask his friends when he returned to the United States. We learned of Calvin's prayer a few weeks after he joined us. We were in awe that God had chosen us to answer such a seemingly impossible prayer!

A year later, Chuck and Tip Reichert, one of the couples helping to support Calvin, took him to Kenya for his brother Rogers' wedding. Tip, the mother of seven, had also fostered seven more. In Kenya, she was drawn to Joash. "He looked so lost," she told me. "He needed a mother."

Joash had been continually moved around between Rogers and relatives. Evan agreed with Tip that maybe Joash could follow Calvin to the United States. "I know this seems crazy," Evan emailed us, "but what would you think about taking Joash in, too?"

Joash had been only eight years old when his mother died. He adored her, and she had always loved and protected him— her youngest. The older boys were more independent, but Joash had always preferred to be at his mother's side.

When she was taken to a separate hut, Joash often sneaked through the window at night to sit by her side. He hoped that his mother would not die, like his dad and so many others in his village.

Joash was at his mother's side only moments before she died. Someone told him to go take a shower, but then he heard loud weeping. He ran back towards the hut. In horror, Joash realized she was gone.

Joash ran to the river to be alone. There, his body shook as he cried. *God must be punishing me*, he thought. *He has taken my mother and left me all alone.* Joash sobbed for hours before a cousin found him. His grandfather took him in for a time, but the gruff old man resented the responsibility. Joash bounced back and forth between relatives and his brother Rogers, who was attending school for masonry and couldn't adequately supervise his younger brother. He was just a teenager himself.

At the airport, five years after his mother died, Joash cried when Calvin left for the United States. He loved his brother very much. One evening, Joash said to Rogers, "I wish Calvin were here."

"Then you better start praying if you want to go to the United States and see Calvin again," Rogers had answered.

That night, before bed, Joash said the first prayer he had ever said on his own. He prayed the Our Father, a prayer he had learned in school. And every night after that, he said an Our Father before going to sleep.

A few months later, Rogers let Joash know that Evan wanted to make arrangements for him to join Calvin. His wish was coming true!

So Joash joined our family. We gradually learned, however, that the loss of his mother affected how he encountered the world. He had developed a defensiveness that followed him to the United States. Very soon after his arrival in July 2005, he began exhibiting very undesirable conduct. We knew his negative behavior was born of pain, but we could not seem to make things better.

After about seven months, Mark and I decided the situation was more than we could handle. On the evening we planned to reveal our plans to find another placement for him, Joash approached us first. "I stopped at the chapel at school today and prayed," he said. "I've asked God to help me. Please give me another chance. I will try harder."

Joash's pledge was salve to my heart. I did not want to send him away—I just wanted a manageable family life. Afterwards, for the first time, instead of grudgingly doing chores, Joash tried to be more helpful. He also studied harder. What mattered to us was that he was trying, but I also noticed something else. When one of the younger children was upset about something or sullen, Joash comforted them. He would try to stop their tears or just talk with them and suggest a fun activity. It was clear that this boy had built a wall around a very big heart.

Then Joash made an amazing discovery that dramatically changed his life. After lackluster seasons in soccer and basketball, track began. Joash had once tried to run a race in sixth grade but quit when some kids laughed after he tripped. In eighth grade, he entered a race and seemed to be off to a good start, running past everyone. Unfortunately, he was soon pulled out and disqualified; he hadn't realized that it was a walking race.

As a freshman at St. Mary's, he tried track one more time. That's when he discovered that he could run—fast! At one meet, I listened to the crowd yell: "Go, Joash, go!" When he crossed the finish line in first place, tears came to my eyes—not because he had won, but because his victory was far more than just a foot race. He was becoming confident and happy.

At the end of his freshman season, after running for only three months, Joash took seventh at state for the 1600 meter and fourth in the 3200 meter. At the end of his first cross-country season as a sophomore, Joash was the second fastest runner on the 5K course—a mere four seconds behind the winner. In his junior and senior year, he took first place.

During his senior cross-country season, Joash broke every course record except one. In his senior year, at the Nike National race in Portland, Oregon, Joash came in third against 199 of the fastest runners in the country.

This boy, who once struggled at home and school, received a five-year full-ride running scholarship and was awarded Academic All American during his freshman year of college. Joash eventually hopes to become an U.S. citizen and work in the medical field. Calvin graduated from University of Mary in respiratory therapy and will graduate from medical school. His goal is to one day open a clinic in Kenya.

These two brothers from Kenya brought much unexpected joy and adventure into our lives. They became our sons; they became brothers to our other children. Most of all, they expanded our hearts.

THE SIBLING BOND

Theresa Kloska Thomas

LAST WEEK MY oldest son David left the house to be measured for his high-school graduation cap and gown. He looked so strong and handsome and sure of himself as he walked out the door with his sweatshirt slung over his shoulder and his keys jingling in his hands.

I can hardly believe he's almost eighteen! What happened to the little boy I brought home from the hospital in the white ducky snowsuit that was two sizes too big?

That same week my youngest daughter, Angela, began sitting up and eating solid food. At five months old, she's been in our family for her entire lifetime, but that's only a semester in my older son's world. It really was almost yesterday when we brought her home in her delicate pink gown on a warm summer evening.

These two kids are a generation apart. Angela is entering this family's daily life, and in a way, David is exiting. She's just getting to know our faces and voices; he's ready to exchange them for new ones. What kind of relationship, you may wonder, can these two siblings have, being so many years and worlds apart?

It's just past 7:00 PM. Football practice ended half an hour ago, and David and his brother Michael walk through the door with hearty appetites and mountains of homework. I hear the door creak and the thump of equipment hitting the floor. Next I hear David's husky voice cooing, "Come on, baby" to his little sister, whom he has rescued from the swing in the front room.

I peek around the corner just in time to see her respond by grabbing his face and wiggling towards him. "Shh... shh... shh..." he says, as he cradles her in his arms and bounces her gently back and forth, holding her securely against his chest. Back and forth, back and forth—they are engaged in a dance, two unlikely companions frozen in a single moment. For a short time they will be under the same roof, in the same world. Then suddenly, their lives will diverge into strikingly separate paths—hers of blocks and ABCs and babyhood, his of college term papers, interviews, and adulthood. But for now, they are in the same plane. She is learning from his strong arms to trust. He is learning from her vulnerability to give. He is a father of tomorrow, in an internship of sorts, learning gentleness and devotion from this little bundle called Sister.

In a minute, David sets Angela down and resumes his teen-age cares, heading to the refrigerator to look for pizza, an apple, or some leftover dinner. Will he remember this moment? Probably not. Will she? Even less likely. But the bonds that have been forged run deep, even if the individual moment is forgotten. Link by link, the family chain lengthens and strengthens. Angela will be closer in age to David's children than to her own brother. Most likely she will play with her nieces and her nephews as if they were her siblings.

What do these siblings offer each other? David gives Angela security, protection, and unconditional love. Angela gives David the opportunity to learn that gentleness is strength. Because of David, Angela has more than just her father to provide a reference in her mind for understanding a gentle, all-loving, protective God. And David won't need a teacher in catechism class to tell him that there is value and beauty in every stage of life. He already knows that, because he lived with Angela.

THE GIFT I FEARED

Thomas G. Mahala

"IT'S A GIRL!" the nurse announced. After the birth of seven healthy sons, those words should have brought great joy. Under different circumstances, I would have done back flips. Instead, as I caught a glimpse of my daughter's face, I scrutinized her eyes. When I saw her almond-shaped eyes, my heart froze—Down syndrome.

My wife Bonnie was forty-six years old. We knew that the likelihood of a baby with Down syndrome increases with maternal age. The possibility was a constant and mostly unspoken thought that had hung over this pregnancy. We were not in denial but rather in rejection. Our prayers were for a healthy child. A special needs child was for some other family; one that was stronger and holier than ours.

Our handsome, intelligent, and athletically gifted sons brought us great joy and not a little pride. We did not want to endure the opinions of others who felt that we should have used contraception or quit while we were ahead. I even imagined certain members of our family members saying, "Why didn't you leave well enough alone when you already had seven healthy children?"

Today, tragically, nine out of ten babies with Down syndrome are aborted. Bonnie and I are passionately pro-life. We chose not to do ultrasounds or prenatal testing. Only after giving birth to a set of twins did Bonnie agree to an ultrasound during this time, just to be sure there was only one baby in there. The fact that everything seemed to be fine gave us hope that this pregnancy would not result in a child with Down syndrome.

Just months earlier, as the summer of 2008 came to an end, Bonnie and I were torn between being thankful that the long hot, New Jersey summer with our seven sons (ranging in age from fifteen years old to two) and its corresponding chaos was over and dreading the back-to-school franticness that lay ahead. Transitioning into back-to-school mode, the fall brought all the usual activities: baseball, parent/teacher conferences, pinewood derbies, cooler weather, and the start of football season. Near Halloween, we also faced the birth of our eighth child, due the first week of November 2008.

After having seven sons in a row with no girls, everyone seemed interested in the outcome of this pregnancy. Two questions seemed never ending: "Still trying for a girl?" and "Are you done yet?"

I liked to answer, "No, we stopped trying for a girl four boys ago!" Bonnie often answered, "No, I think we'll try for a few more boys, and *then* we'll start trying for a girl!" These conversations would inevitably close with the comment, "...as long as the baby is healthy."

Health was important to us. We were silently fearful by the thought of having a child with Down syndrome. Friends of ours, former neighbors and the husband of a work colleague of mine, had given birth to their seventh son in 2006. His name was John Paul, and he was born with Down syndrome. We had an uncanny number of things in common with these friends, but this was one thing we hoped not to share with them.

The Friday morning Bonnie went into labor, I woke up with the worst toothache of my life. Luckily, I was able to get into the dentist for an emergency surgical procedure that included a root canal and removing a small portion of my jawbone. I was given a prescription for a painkiller to use when the novocaine wore off. When I returned home, Bonnie had to return three extra visiting children to their own homes and then start dinner before announcing she would pack her bag—code word for, "It's time!"

This means I can't take the pain medicine, I thought, realizing I needed to drive and be on my toes for the next several hours. It crossed my mind that God was assisting me to "die to self." Bonnie would have the pain of labor to offer up in union with Christ's suffering, and I, too, would have pain to offer up for my family and a safe delivery.

Bonnie's labor was one of her easiest. The doctor and nurses acted swiftly amid an atmosphere of anticipation. The nurse and I cheered Bonnie through the contractions and pushing. The baby slipped out after one big push. But after her arrival, the atmosphere turned tense and quiet. I tried to mask my emotions. What kind of a father would express disappointment and even rejection for his own daughter? I knew it was wrong to feel that way.

Feigning happiness was beyond my acting ability, so instead I tried miserably to hide my emotions. Bonnie looked searchingly into my eyes. She hadn't seen the baby who had just been whisked away. The absence of joyful excitement and a pensive look on my face told Bonnie what she was wondering—this was the baby we had feared that God would give us. The wait was over. Now we knew. Bonnie silently wept.

My heart cried for an announcement from the nurses: "Everything's fine—she's perfect!" There was none. Our doctor confirmed that our baby seemed to have Down syndrome and explained that she needed tests done on her heart. (More than half of children who have Down syndrome are born with cardiac conditions.)

After being examined by a pediatric cardiologist, we were told that our daughter had two holes in her heart, known as an atrioventricular canal defect. She would have to undergo open-heart surgery when she was a few months older. Instead of anguish, the news prompted a somber reflection: *If she dies as a result of her surgery, the pain will be over for all of us.* Those were not thoughts we were proud of, but they were the ones we had.

We hadn't even named her yet. Bonnie looked at me and said, "Let's call her Grace Anne." She wanted something pretty yet simple, already thinking of the learning challenges that would lie ahead. I agreed immediately. Only much later would the relevance of her name have greater meaning to me.

I left the hospital at 3:00 AM in a daze. I welcomed the privacy of my car where I could finally let the tears flow. I cried the entire half-hour ride home.

Our other children were still asleep, so I rolled into bed, physically and emotionally exhausted. Upon waking from a short and restless sleep, the previous night seemed like a bad dream until reality pushed into my consciousness, filling me with the dreaded realization all over again. It felt as though God had played a mean trick on us. *Be open to life, accept seven sons, accept a pregnancy later in life and then, I will give you a daughter, but she will have a disability.*

Besides the anguish of a disabled daughter was the anguish that I felt such little love in my heart for her. My pleading to God began. *Lord, please help me to love my daughter the way you do.* I knew it was wrong not to love her the way I loved my sons. I began a relentless pursuit to learn to love like God loves.

The first task before me was how to tell the boys about their new sister. Bonnie had sent an email to several friends and also to a prayer chain, asking for prayers as our little girl had a serious heart condition. She asked people to pray for "grace" to guide us on this journey. I shared the email with our older sons. As they finished reading it, we cried and hugged each other.

"You would think that getting an extra chromosome would be a good thing," my oldest son Thomas commented, "like scoring one more run in a game." We discussed how to respond to people with questions about Grace. It didn't seem right to say, "We have a girl, but she has Down syndrome." We decided it would be best to just say that our new baby was a girl, and if anyone asked how she was doing, we would then explain, "She has a heart issue, which is very common for babies born with Down syndrome."

I told the older boys, "Guys, the world often defines a person as 'perfect' when he or she is pretty, handsome, athletic, intelligent, and wealthy. Yet, these are not the qualities that God judges us on. He looks at our souls because it is the pure souls that experience the eternal glory of heaven." I used the example of Mother Teresa, someone who did not fit the stereotype of physical beauty but was beautiful to God and on her way to sainthood.

I felt that the Holy Spirit gave me words to comfort my sons. "Maybe God knew our family wanted a girl, so he is telling us, 'I didn't want to send just any girl. I saved the *perfect* girl for your family. This little girl has an incorruptible soul!'" The kids were quiet and appeared to absorb what I was saying. "Think of what a gift it is to have her living under our own roof," I continued. "To be able to love her is to love God! You see, God knows what is best for all of us!"

I was amazed at how easily those words came to me, but I was disappointed that my love for my daughter was not coming as easily. Why couldn't I love her the way she is? Why couldn't I be as happy about her as my younger sons were? I simply told them that they had a sister and her name was Grace. They went bananas, jumping up and down. "It's a girl, it's a girl!" they yelled. *Lord, help me to love like these little ones,* I prayed.

After Grace and Bonnie returned from the hospital, managing six school-aged boys and one toddler became more complicated with the new set of routines for Grace. She required physical and occupational therapy twice a week, along with monthly visits to her cardiologist. The shock of Grace's birth and her diagnosis began to wear off, although Bonnie and I continued to struggle with loving her unconditionally. One night we cried together and shared our disappointments. "You have your boys. You have your baseball team," Bonnie cried, "but I don't have my daughter."

"I wanted a daughter I could walk down the aisle at her wedding," I cried. "She'll never get married." The evil one continued to work on me by making me feel that I was robbed of a perfect daughter, and I feared that I would never be able to really love her. I responded by seeking prayers and guidance from faith-filled friends and those who had children with Down syndrome.

As Grace approached five months old and her impending open-heart surgery, mixed emotions plagued me. I was less nervous about this major surgery than I would have been if it had been one of my sons. *Lord, please have mercy on me,* I prayed, not wanting to love Grace any less than my other children. In a very subtle way, a feeling of compassion for our little Grace flickered in my heart. She weighed only ten pounds—so little to face a life-threatening surgery.

A few days before her surgery, I reflected on the day's gospel and read a reflection on our Lord's unconditional love. The simple reality of loving unconditionally took hold of me. As I held Grace in my arms, it hit me that focusing on her "condition" was preventing me from giving her my entire heart. I was seeing with worldly eyes, with limited vision. Christ sees us through his Sacred Heart, and I began to understand that Christ wanted me to love Grace *unconditionally*—to be blind to her condition.

Bonnie had already reached that point. In fact, as she realized that our culture would not affect Grace in the same way as other girls, she began to see the advantage of having a daughter with Down syndrome. On the day of her surgery, Bonnie could not bear to be the one to hand her over to the medical staff.

As I held Grace in the early morning hours prior to her surgery and then eventually walked down the hall to the operating room with her, my heart swelled with emotion. I was falling in love. Suddenly, I couldn't imagine losing my baby girl. My heart ached for the pain Grace would go through. When I laid her on that operating table and they began to administer anesthesia, I prayed and cried for my little angel. I didn't want to lose her!

Grace came out of surgery with a seven-inch scar down the center of her chest. The holes in her heart had been repaired. When she came home from the hospital, she began to emerge as the heart of our family, and the holes in our hearts were also repaired. Her little personality began to captivate us, and all the boys fell deeply in love with their little sister. They do treat Grace differently than they treat each other, and I believe it's because, through Grace, our hearts have grown. Her brothers constantly hug and kiss her and tell her they love her. Our boys might be gifted athletically, but Grace, who cannot even run or jump, is gifted in love.

One night at dinner, my son Patrick, who was eight years old at the time, told us that one of his classmates said that he felt sorry for Grace because she would grow up to look funny. Ten-year-old Jack responded, "Patrick, you have to tell him that when we die, our bodies don't go to heaven—only our souls do, so God only sees the soul!" Such wisdom from one so young, thanks to Grace!

A recent event in our family showed us even more how fleeting physical perfection is. Our oldest son had a brain aneurism rupture two days before his high-school graduation. For nineteen days, my son, who planned to attend the Naval Academy, clung to life in a neuro-intensive care unit. Thankfully, he recovered. During his recovery, after waking from a coma, we asked him if there was anything he wanted us to bring him from home. "Just bring Grace," he said.

Every night when I get home from work, I am greeted by hugs and kisses from Grace, who is now three years old. I am the luckiest man on the face of the earth because of her, and for me to utter those words is truly a miracle. I tell people today that if God told me he had made a mistake and needed to reverse her Down syndrome condition, I would say, "No thank you—she's perfect!

Bonnie and I thank God for sending Grace to heal our own special needs. We cannot imagine wanting any other little girl more than her.

LEARNING TO BE BIG HEARTED

Kate Coates

IT WAS LATE summer 1996 when I sat down to breakfast with my oldest friend. We were nineteen, and our lives—once so intertwined—had taken divergent paths over the last twelve months. I wondered if she knew just *how* divergent. She turned her cup over to indicate she wanted coffee, teasing me when I didn't follow suit.

"Turning over a new leaf?" she asked, smiling.

"No. Just don't want coffee, I guess."

"What? That's what we drink! Are you okay?"

"Just trying to stop drinking caffeine."

"Hey—It's not that bad for you! I mean, it's not like you're *pregnant* or something."

I was speechless.

I grew up in a strong Catholic home, the eldest daughter in a family of six children. Happy as a child, I struggled through adolescence when the good grades my father expected of me became harder to achieve. As I progressed through high school, I sought solace from my troubles in friendships with people who were worse off than I was. Helping them made me feel better. When I met the father of my child, he had just come through a very difficult period in his life. As time went on, we fell in love, and together, we made a series of bad decisions. Though I hadn't believed in sex before marriage, I allowed myself to think it was "okay" because I was sure he was the one for me.

Learning I was pregnant at nineteen was terrifying. When Ryan and I suspected it, we couldn't even say the words out loud. Fearing our parents' rage and disappointment, we talked about taking all the money we had and just driving as far as we could.

In reality, we were very blessed by the way our parents handled the situation. Though the months to come would see a fair amount of disagreements, yelling, and tears, both sets of parents reacted supportively when we shared the news. My father was calm and told me not to rush down the aisle. While my mother couldn't speak to me for three days, she told me it was not the pregnancy that upset her; she believed that the baby was a gift from God. It was the act that led to the baby that left her so distraught.

When friends and family learned I was expecting, it seemed they all wanted to give me advice. Some friends suggested we get married; some made crude jokes. A cousin laughed and said we'd never last. Most assumed that we would keep the baby. Ryan asked for my hand in marriage—he wanted to be a father to our child.

But after the storm of sharing the news had settled, I found myself having doubts. I needed a break; I needed to think. My mom, initially so shaken, became a wonderful support to me. She shared every resource she could find with me: she put me in touch with Catholic Charities, and she discovered a maternity home a few hours away. Together, we visited the place, and I saw the other pregnant girls who lived there. In addition to parenting classes, the home offered counseling to the residents about whether or not to keep their babies. My mom made it clear she was in no way pressuring me to give up the baby for adoption; whatever I decided had to be my choice since I was the one who would have to live with it. After praying about it, I knew it was where I should be. It would mean having the baby in a hospital three hours from home; I couldn't imagine Ryan agreeing to it. That night, my mom and I drove home, my stomach in knots.

The next day, Ryan and I talked. I explained to him that, while I felt so supported, I also felt lost and confused about my own feelings. I was unsure that I was strong enough or ready to be a mother. I told him how all the voices and opinions of everyone around me had become a din I felt I couldn't escape, and I needed to get away and let my own voice rise to the surface. I was edified when he gave me his blessing.

After arriving at St. Elizabeth's, I was given a room and taught the ropes. The home kept a strict schedule of chores and classes. Each girl had assigned duties and took turns doing weekly tasks, such as unloading the box truck that brought our food or planning and preparing meals. I met my fellow residents, who ranged in age from fourteen to nineteen. Most of them were wards of the state, having no choice but to reside there. I learned that, rather than giving up their babies, most girls kept them and then moved to St. Elizabeth's sister residence: a home for single teen mothers and their children. I felt strangely alone in a home full of peers, and yet in a way that was just what I'd come for.

In the weeks that followed, I learned the skills I would need if I planned to keep my child and live on my own. I learned which bus to board to get downtown. I learned how to clean a house—as well as a baby—from top to bottom. I learned how to make my mom's tuna casserole. I discovered that one of my housemates had had four abortions before her current pregnancy. I wrote letter after letter to Ryan, family, and friends. I found a job. I went on Medicaid. I got lice.

But of all the things I learned in my time there, above all I learned how blessed and fortunate I was. My housemates had so very little—I saw that the day I walked in the door. What I didn't realize then was that the gift I truly had that they were lacking had nothing to do with money. I was blessed, above all, with *love*. So many of the girls I lived with walked in a world of darkness. Their default reaction to a greeting was always cold and hard, because they hadn't known much—if any—love. The longer I stayed there, the more humbled I was by my blessings, and the greater my desire to return to my family.

I was home by Thanksgiving, grateful to be able to return to my old job at a store downtown. As the days passed, I grew closer to making a decision about whether or not to keep the baby. I felt no pressure to give the baby up; in fact, Ryan was firmly against the idea, determined that if he had a child living in the world he would be his father. I was, quite simply, scared. I had attended one semester of college before dropping out to waitress at a diner. I had been aimless and searching. All I'd ever wanted to be was a wife and a mother. Yet here I was pregnant, and so unsure of myself. I didn't feel worthy.

Furthermore, I believed that Ryan and I would be married one day. However, we'd always assumed we would marry when we graduated college and began our careers, not at nineteen or twenty. Ryan was ready and willing to marry me, but I felt so immature, and I felt that he was, too. We'd never talked about adult issues. We knew we believed in the same things, but we had never discussed money management, or who would do household repairs. I couldn't really put my finger on it, but I just knew we weren't ready yet. I was worried that there were differences we had yet to uncover. For instance, I was Catholic, but Ryan was not. I worried that simple things might mean bigger problems once we were married—like the fact that his room was always a mess.

By Christmas, I knew I was meant to keep my baby. Advent was deeply meaningful as I identified with the Blessed Mother as an unwed, pregnant girl. The moments I spent at Mass were intimate and peaceful as I felt our Lord drawing me close. I asked him to bless my baby. Changes came as Advent turned to Ordinary Time. My parents, who supported me and quietly assented to my decision to keep my child, told me that they believed it would be best if I found an apartment. They told me that, although they were behind me, I needed to do this on my own.

Ryan and I attended St. Vincent's, a church across town from the ones each of us had grown up in. We met with a dear priest there named Fr. Joe, who listened to our story and agreed to place us in the marriage prep program even though we weren't engaged. We took a test that helped us learn about our similarities and differences, and we met with our sponsors, a couple who guided us in discerning whether or not we were meant to marry. Ryan was patient with me as I worked through things.

My counselor at Catholic Charities assisted me to set up a budget so I could live independently. Once we figured out what I could afford to spend on rent, I began searching for an apartment. Ryan, who was working and going to school, told me he intended to help pay the rent. We would not live together, engaged or not, but he felt it was his duty to help shelter his child. When a grocery store in town went out of business, I stocked up on non-perishables, cooking supplies, and sundries for my "future" apartment. I circled ads in the paper, and then found the perfect place to live through friends of Ryan's family—another blessing. I moved in February 1st. Generous coworkers gave me furniture, kitchen utensils, an old television set, and a highchair. My dad bought a totaled car at a sheriff's auction and fixed it up, allowing me to buy it from him by making monthly payments. I was set. Now all I had to do was wait.

The eighth month of my pregnancy was the hardest. One day, I walked to the bakery to pick up lunch for my coworkers downtown, in awe of my size and self-conscious of my naked ring finger. What was I doing? How did I get here? This was not the way I had envisioned becoming a mother. I felt like such a failure. Waiting there in line, I was surprised when the little old lady in front of me turned around. Her hunched back caused her gaze to fall on my swollen womb, and she smiled immediately. Looking up at me, her eyes twinkled as she said, "Oh, how I envy you!" God reminded me of his gift.

I was a kid having a kid. I was not only scared of what the reality of parenting would bring but also terrified of the pain. I knew I had no right to complain, but one day near the end of my pregnancy, my eyes welled up with tears and I told my mom how I felt like I'd been pulled off the sidelines and thrown into a game of basketball and told that I had to make the winning shot, whether I liked it or not—and I didn't even play basketball! She responded with love, looking me in the eyes and telling me that I only needed to remember that I was joining centuries of women who had done the same thing while biting on sticks, and I could do it too.

In early March, sleeping in the twin bed in my apartment, I awoke to a sharp pain in my abdomen, accompanied by a gush. It was 3:43 AM. I experienced contractions for the next hour and a half. When I called Ryan, he came right over and drove me to the hospital where we would await the arrival of what I assumed was our son (though in my heart I hoped for a girl). I was blessed with a beautiful natural delivery and the announcement that it was a girl! I couldn't stop kissing her through my tears.

On May 11, 1997, Ryan arrived early to help me prepare the apartment for the party that would follow Emma's baptism later that day. It was my first Mother's Day as well. He took me outside, presumably to show me a huge flock of geese that he'd seen, and then handed me my Mother's Day card. It read, "Happy Mother's Day to My Wife...will you marry me?" I was overcome with joy.

Ryan and I were married when our daughter was five-and-a-half months old. The years since have been filled with joys as well as struggles. With each day that passes, we are enriched by the five beautiful lives God has entrusted to our care, and we know without a doubt that the greatest gift we can give them is love. Through it all, and with the love and support of our families and the Church, God has taught us how to become a big-hearted family.

WE WILL LOVE YOU FOREVER

Calvin Bader

"YOU ARE NOT ovulating," the doctor told my wife, Donna. That explained why we were unable to start a family. Although we were still in our early twenties and had been married just a little over a year, we both wanted children right away. We knew couples that had poured thousands of dollars into fertility treatments, and neither of us wanted to go that route.

In spite of our disappointment, we recovered quickly from the news. Donna and I had been doing foster care for an adoption agency—caring for infants until they were placed with families—so adoption was an easy choice for us. In addition, my mother had provided foster care from the time I was eleven years old, and two of the five children in our family were adopted. Donna and I prayed and trusted God to guide our way.

It was a Friday that we learned of Donna's infertility. By Monday, she called me at work. "Calvin, we're parents!" she cried.

"What do you mean?" I asked. Donna explained that we could adopt two-week-old Samuel, a baby my mother had been fostering. The original adoptive family backed out, and since we were already licensed with the agency as foster parents, they agreed to let us adopt him.

It was a surreal moment. I came home from work and hugged Donna. "We're parents!" I cried. I kept thinking, *Is this really happening?* It seemed too good to be true. We thanked God for the amazing gift of our beautiful little Samuel as we joyfully took on our new role as parents. But God was not finished building our family yet.

Shortly after we adopted Samuel, Donna and I applied to work for Noah's Ark Children's Village, an agency on eighty-eight acres with several on-site foster homes. It was designed so that mothers can stay at home and fathers can still hold an outside job. While we were waiting to be hired, Donna and I were asked to work as substitutes for a set of regular houseparents who would be leaving Noah's Ark soon. It was the perfect way for us to get a feel for the job.

Although the first time we substituted was only for two hours, it was an eye-opening experience. Looking back on my childhood, I realized that I had been oblivious to the extent of the responsibility required to care for foster children coming from all kinds of backgrounds. The five children we cared for that day were young and needed a lot of attention, but I felt called to this important work. I was not so sure about Donna. She cried the whole way home. I did not say anything at first. *Why is she crying?* I wondered. *Did she get attached to the kids? Is this going to be too hard for her?*

When I asked Donna what was wrong, her answer took me

by surprise. "I know Dylan is supposed to be our son," she cried. Dylan was a little blonde-haired boy who looked much younger than his three years of age. He still wore diapers and did not speak much beyond grunts. Instead of talking, he used hitting to communicate. Toddlers are usually happy and curious, but Dylan was neither. Instead, his eyes reflected deep sadness. This was his fourth foster home. Although we did our best to get Dylan to warm up to us, he had ignored us completely.

The plan was for Donna and me to take over for the current houseparents once they left. I would continue my day job as a radio engineer. In order for us to become licensed for Noah's Ark, though, all the children would be placed elsewhere. An on-site home study was required, and only after that was completed could we begin accepting children.

"Dylan has be to placed in another home," I pointed out to her.

"I don't care," she responded. "He *is* going to be our son." I thought she was overreacting, but yet something in her spirit had to be driving such strong feelings. A few days later, the agency called us to babysit for an entire weekend for the same family. Dylan continued to ignore us. To make matters worse, some of the kids, including Dylan, were sick and had diarrhea the whole time. On the drive home, Donna was in tears again. "I know Dylan is supposed to be our son," she insisted.

"Parental rights have not been terminated, so he's not even *available* for adoption," I reasoned. Donna admitted it did not make sense, but she felt certain that God had led us to Dylan and that one day he would be our son.

I did not have an emotional connection to Dylan, so I was thinking logically.

"Well, try not to get your hopes up," I told her. I figured we would just move forward and eventually, Donna would accept that it was not possible for us to adopt him.

A few months later, we moved into one of the Noah's Ark homes and began taking in foster children. Dylan was placed in another home on the premises, but it was not long before his personality clashed with the foster parents. He had pushed a two-year-old down some stairs, knocked other kids down, and was still not talking. His only words, which he said over and over, were "truck" and "blue." Even before our licensing was complete, Dylan often spent time with us during the day. Once the licensing was approved, everyone agreed it was best to move him back into our home. During this time, in spite of his violence with other toddlers, there was never a concern for Samuel's safety. He only lashed out among peers trying to play with him.

Looking at Dylan, you would think he was a sweet little blonde-haired toddler, but he had built a wall around himself due to early emotional trauma. The hitting and inability to communicate continued. He was diagnosed as autistic due to repetitive behaviors such as rocking and hypersensitivity to fabric and noise.

Donna never wavered in believing that we would adopt him. Once Dylan began spending time with us on a daily basis, the idea of becoming his father began to take hold of me. *I guess this is going to happen,* I started thinking. *He's going to become our son.* Parental rights still had not been severed, but I stopped wondering how it would happen and just felt like Donna that he would become our son.

A few months later, parental rights were terminated, and we immediately began the adoption process. While God seemed to be leading us in this direction, Dylan gave us no encouragement. Often when he was upset and Donna tried to soothe him, he would react by screaming at her. Donna just kept showering him with love and patience, and little by little, he started responding. The first time Dylan crawled up onto Donna's lap, we looked at each other and smiled; our eyes met in silent celebration. Still, he ignored my existence.

I was trying to bond with a child who wanted nothing to do with me. It was a challenge I was committed to win. *What can I do to show him that he does not need to be afraid of me?* I wondered. I would sit down and play with toys near him, trying to interest him. Dylan sat near the toys, but turned away so I was out of his sight. He didn't even want to get into the car if I was there. "Dear Lord, please give me the right words to say and the right actions to show I'm here to love not to hurt," I prayed. "Please bring down that wall and allow Dylan to heal."

One day, Donna took Dylan to a playground. Then, while he warmed up and began having fun, I joined them and took Dylan horseback riding. He was so excited about being on a horse that the happiness stayed with him—it was a breakthrough. I trotted alongside beside him with tears of happiness in my eyes at seeing his still-smiling face. After that day, Dylan began trusting me.

We were making progress, but still the grip of pain on Dylan would not let go. For the first four months, not a day went by that Dylan did not act out in some way—throwing tantrums and hitting. Coming home from work and seeing Donna drained from so much emotional stress during the day was hard for me. There were times I wondered if it was too much. "Are you sure you want to continue doing this?" I asked.

Ninety-nine percent of the time, I would think, *We are going to get through it.* But there was a one-percent doubt that sometimes crossed my mind—*Maybe we can't.* As soon as that thought came, I would immediately remember that God had led Dylan to us, and God would give us the strength and resources to raise him.

There were times when Donna herself wondered how she could go on. One day while I was at work, she had put Dylan in a corner for time out. He screamed and banged his head against the wall. Donna put her arms around him. "I love you, Dylan," she cried. "You're safe now. Daddy and I are never going to leave you." Yet, as she said those words, she silently prayed: *God, should we be doing this? Are we in over our heads?* She wondered if she had been mistaken—maybe she was not supposed to be Dylan's mother after all. She sat with Dylan for half an hour before he finally began to calm down. *Dear God, help this to stop,* she prayed. *Help Dylan not to be afraid anymore.* Donna held Dylan and cried with him. She was scared she might not be able to help him, but then she remembered the promise she had made to love him forever.

We both realized that if we did not keep Dylan, who would? In the end, our love for him did not waver. He needed us—we couldn't give up on him. We prayed continually for Dylan to be healed from his bad memories. We also fasted. Our family and church friends joined us in praying for his pain, and many of them fasted, too. We were powerless to help him; it was all in God's hands. We continued to reassure Dylan through our love. We taught him about God, and prayed together as a family every evening.

Gradually, his autistic behaviors began to fade. For instance, Dylan stopped being oversensitive to textures. Before, it could take twenty minutes for him to put his socks on—they just didn't feel right to him. Gradually, though, everything did not always have to be exactly the way he wanted it. Dylan also started saying words.

That first year with Dylan was rough, but after six months he began making rapid progress. It became clear that he was not autistic. By the time his adoption was final, our son was emerging into a happy little four-year-old boy. He went from not wanting to talk or interact with people to smiling and being very outgoing. There were still bad days, but Dylan had let us into his heart and he was firmly in ours.

After a year and a half at Noah's Ark, we moved to Florida for a two-year break to bond as a family without the distractions of caring for so many other children. During our first Christmas in Florida, my bond with Dylan was sealed for me in an unexpected way. We had gotten him a bike for Christmas, and I took him outside to teach him to ride it. After only about three minutes, he was able to ride it alone. It was a bittersweet moment for me. I wanted to hold the seat and help him longer, but he didn't need me. Seeing his ear-to-ear smile, I suddenly felt deep inside me, *I'm really his dad.* It was a rite of passage for me that I had been a part of something so important to him.

We returned to Noah's Ark when Dylan was seven and Samuel was four. The boys were close to each other, and Dylan now felt like he belonged with us. We worked there for another five years. And then, two weeks after leaving Noah's Ark, we received unexpected news: Donna was pregnant! After ten years of marriage God had blessed us with a little girl!

Dylan, at fifteen, is affectionate, outgoing, and loves the outdoors—just like me as a boy. He and Samuel are typical brothers; they hang out together, are best friends until they fight—and then they get over it and are best friends again. Emma, age three, loves to tag along with her brothers. They've both decided that when she is old enough to date, they will be at the door with guns guarding their sister.

Our family has experienced the importance of trusting God's leading. We are teaching our kids to always look for ways to help others—sponsoring another family every Christmas and working at a local soup kitchen every month are two examples. Donna and I teach the kids that since everything we have is a gift from God we need to reach out and share those gifts with others.

CHRISTMAS WITHOUT MONEY

Gae Onions

OUR FAMILY'S MOST cherished season is Advent and Christmas. These holidays are celebrated in a big way in our household, with special prayers, food, decorations—and lots and lots of presents.

But three years ago, our family was experiencing a severe financial trial. Money was tight, and there were no extras. Stephen, my husband, was working away from home, which added travel expenses. Supporting twelve children didn't make anything easier. It was in these circumstances, however, that we discovered the real meaning of Christmas.

How are we going to be able to buy gifts to the standard we have done in the past? I thought. As Christmas drew closer, I sadly realized we would not be able to have many Christmas presents at all for the children. Stephen and I struggled with this idea over the phone, thousands of miles away from each other. We decided to discuss the situation with the children. There simply was no way out of it.

When Stephen came home, we gathered the children

together. "There will be few, if any, presents for Christmas this year," we told them. "We're sorry—it's just the way it is and cannot be helped."

But instead of sad faces, the children surprised us. No one seemed upset and everyone seemed to understand. They were more concerned about whether we were still going to have our Midnight Feast after Midnight Mass. "Are we still going to be able to bake cookies, cakes, and puddings like we usually do?" one of them asked. Another wondered, "Are we going to be able to celebrate the saint feast days during Advent with all our traditions?"

"Yes," I told them. "Family cooking and traditions will continue, although St. Nicholas day will have to be toned down a lot." They all agreed that they would be quite happy celebrating this simple way.

At first I felt relieved, but I began to feel that we were shortchanging the children by not giving them all the gifts we were used to giving them—after all, this was a twenty-two year tradition for us. That's what parents do; give good gifts to their children, right?

Imagine my dismay when I worked out the final math and realized that we could not afford to buy *any* presents for Christmas! My heart sank when I thought about Christmas morning. And this would be our sweet little Arwen's first Christmas. I had a good, long cry and dwelled on this sad predicament with a few good friends who listened patiently.

Finally, I mustered up the courage to tell the children there would be no gifts at all. I wasn't brave enough to do it in a group setting, so I approached them individually. They accepted the news with such understanding and good cheer that only God could have prepared their hearts. Their amazing attitudes filled me with gratitude. Once again they brought up the question of traditions and food, and once again I reassured them that we could definitely do those things, but nothing else. I thanked God for such extraordinary children.

And then it struck me: Christmas to our children wasn't about the presents. Christmas was about the birth of our Lord and the traditions and family times we had created to celebrate this. This truly was an eye-opener. I had never seen Christmas and its meaning through their eyes before. It was humbling. Yet little did I know, the excitement was just beginning.

As I pondered the children's responses, I had an idea. "What if, using materials we already have on hand, everyone *made* a bunch of presents together, and then Daddy and I could distribute them on Christmas morning?"

The kids loved it! We all began working together with a "Santa's Toyshop" theme. It was an old-fashioned, creative Christmas where no one was certain whose gift he or she was making. The idea of not knowing if you were making your own present was fun, too.

We even created a Christmas workshop. We brought raw materials into our library room and set up workstations. We called ourselves Poor Box Toys Inc., an idea from a Robin Hood movie where Friar Tuck tells the Sheriff that he steals money from the poor box in church. The kids made a sign and placed it outside the door with a running worksheet to keep track of what was being made. The children asked me to design laminated badges to wear while in the workshop. Except for purchasing a couple of lengths of pine for some woodworking, we only used what we had on hand. Enthusiasm was building!

My heart lightened as I helped them with their crafts—a bit of glue here, a stitch there. I listened to their lively conversations and saw them grow closer as siblings. We spent many lovely days working on these homemade gifts. Soon, our basket of special presents had grown to near overflowing.

Even as we were happily making presents, our financial situation was becoming even tighter. Our two oldest boys had been begging for our permission to go and find some work to help with the finances. For days, Stephen and I resisted. We felt that we should be providing for them, not having them work for us. Circumstances being what they were, however, we finally agreed.

Having our boys in the workforce eased our financial burden a bit. It meant that we were able to allow a small gift-buying quota for each person in the family. I cannot describe the joy and satisfaction those boys felt as they each brought home a paycheck that was put toward the Christmas gifts.

I will treasure the memories of that Christmas for the rest of my life. From the scraps we had collected around the house, many treasures emerged. The children crafted marionettes, felted mice, paper dolls with clothes, spinning tops from cardboard, food made out of felt for the younger children's play kitchens, bookmarks, and embroidered pictures.

Our children had opened their hearts to the true meaning of Christmas: love and sacrifice for others. They learned that joy comes from giving of themselves, in making and receiving gifts out of love. It warmed my heart to see the virtue in my children—a great gift for this mother.

FAMILY ON THE ROCKS

DeeAnn Smith

IT WAS MY most memorable Mother's Day.

The night before, I had driven my sixteen-year-old daughter to an overnight party at a classmate's ranch in South Texas. My husband came home a little early so he could make dinner and spend the evening with our other four children. When we arrived at the ranch, my daughter bolted out the car door, eager to join her friends. I went inside the house to say hello to the parents who would be chaperoning the party. They were uncorking one of my favorite white wines and asked if I would like to join them. Of course I would!

What these lovely, hospitable ladies did not know was that I am an alcoholic. At that time, I was in denial. There was no such thing as one glass of wine for me. There were two, three, four—only to wake up the next morning and find that I had become an unintended and uninvited guest at my daughter's party.

There is a point in time that recovering alcoholics and addicts refer to as "rock bottom"—a place so hopeless, so desperate, and so lonely that one feels one can't go any lower. This was my rock bottom.

As my daughter drove us home that morning—on Mother's Day, no less—she looked straight ahead. The silence was more unbearable than my self-inflicted shame and throbbing headache. And now it wasn't just my shame anymore; it had become hers, too. I sank into the passenger seat and stared out the window. *If she never forgives me, I would not blame her,* I thought. *I couldn't imagine ever forgiving myself, either.*

I drank too much when I was a teenager and all through my college years, so much so that I would get into all kinds of trouble. I promised my mother and father over and over that I would never drink again. I told myself that when I met the man I would marry and have children with, I would stop drinking.

Fortunately, I was sober for almost a year when I met my husband. The reason, however, was that I had been pregnant for nine months of that year and was now a single mom with an infant daughter.

For the first several years of our marriage, I did not drink. Then, after the birth of our twin boys, who were our fourth and fifth children, I started "drinking socially," enjoying a glass of wine or a frozen margarita when David and I went out to dinner. As the years passed, though, I lacked the willpower to stop at two. In fact, I often had two glasses of wine before even arriving at some social event, only to drink more once I arrived. I was a "high-functioning" alcoholic. After my mother passed away in 2006, my drinking increased.

"I can't believe you did this to me!" my daughter cried, while I lay on the couch that Mother's Day. "Were you drunk when you were driving me there?"

Unbelievably, I had been. I said nothing.

"I'm so humiliated! All my friends were there! My own mother—drunk!"

My husband tried his best to calm our daughter. After so many years of co-dependency, he instinctively responded by trying to protect my foolish behavior. My oldest daughter, who was awakened by the volume in the house, shuffled into the kitchen to make a bowl of cereal and quickly returned to her room. My fifteen-year-old son, who was enjoying a rare weekend opportunity to sleep in, remained in his room as if he could stay asleep through all of the shouting. Our eleven-year-old twin boys sat on two chairs opposite of my couch of shame. And then, the clincher: "Happy Mother's Day," they said.

Hearing those words was as deafening as the sound of a barreling freight train screeching to a halt. It hit me: Our family was on a runaway train headed toward certain disaster. I had to do something to save my family, but first I had to save myself. I didn't want to be a sad, sick, and guilt-ridden woman anymore. I wanted to be the mother that God intended me to be! He had blessed me with these children. It was time to earn back my children's trust. I got up from the couch and opened my laptop. I typed "treatment for alcoholism" into the search engine. It only took one phone call, and within thirty-six hours, I would be on a plane headed to a rehabilitation treatment facility in California, where I would spend the next thirty-three days.

I asked my husband if he supported my decision to get help, and he replied with a resounding "Yes!" We discussed how everything would work at home while I was away. David could use vacation days to take some time off work. We told his mother about the situation, and she agreed to spend a week or two at our house, and cook some of her beloved Nana meals. A dear friend also agreed to be on standby.

I gathered our children together. My choking sorrow and paralyzing fear was replaced with peace and resolve. I looked into the faces that were so dear to me. "I'm going to get help," I told them. "I am addicted to alcohol, and I'm going to a hospital that can help me." Everyone listened silently. "I want to get healthy so I can be a better mother." Tears welled up in me. "I love you all so much." Soon, everyone was crying as we hugged and kissed one another.

Then, my daughter turned the worst Mother's Day of my life into the best. "This Mother's Day is extra special, Mama," she said, her big brown eyes shooting straight into my soul. "This is going to be the best gift you could ever get!"

When she whispered those words to me on Mother's Day in 2009, I was preoccupied with the enormity of the task that loomed ahead, but her words were prophetic.

Alcoholics come up with a variety of reasons why they won't get help for their addiction. There are always reasons that it's inconvenient, but people usually avoid it because it is life-altering work. Admitting one has a problem is one thing, but doing something about it is quite another. The only way an alcoholic is able to begin this journey is to turn his or her life over to a Higher Power.

An often-quoted mantra of AA is, "Let go and let God." Hour by hour, day by day, I gradually let go of the white-knuckled grip of addiction through the gift of God's abundant grace, a gift he keeps on giving!

Gifts come in all shapes and sizes, and often the gifts most appreciated are the ones that are created out of love. Mothers treasure the art-class macaroni necklaces and picture frames glued together with Popsicle sticks lovingly created by their children. But our children give us other gifts that can't be worn around our necks or taped on refrigerator doors. These rare gifts are carefully chosen, freely given, and filled with love. The gift I treasure most from my children is the gift of forgiveness.

The most difficult part of my recovery was learning to forgive myself. There are still moments when a foreboding sense of shame and guilt find a way of sneaking into my subconscious, reawakening the memory of a woman I no longer am and never want to be again. But because I know that God and my family have forgiven me, I, too, can and must forgive myself. It has taken time and trust, patience and practice for all of us.

Getting better and stronger is a family affair. It requires an ongoing willingness to be open to a lifetime of learning, an ongoing choice to love. We cannot totally erase our past, but neither do we have to cover it up. Instead, I've learned to acknowledge my mistakes, ask for forgiveness, forgive others, and move on. In the midst of all of the hurt and healing, my family decided to love, and this was a choice without limits or conditions.

I realized that our children had reached a profound understanding of unconditional love one Sunday evening, in the early days of my recovery, when we gathered for our weekly family meeting. The discussion centered around an upcoming anniversary marking the passing of my mother, their grandmother. We had loved her very much and still missed her. I thought this would be an opportune teaching moment to share how I had learned it was wrong to self-medicate when I felt sad.

"Mama, we forgive you," one of my twin boys assured me.

And then the other twin chimed in, "Like Nana B used to say, 'There's nothing you could ever do that would make me un-love you.'"

JEWELS IN OUR LIFE

Kathy Charley

AN OLD PROVERB states: "A house with a grandparent harbors a jewel." I've been fortunate to learn firsthand how true this is. However, making the decision to care for my elderly parents began only after my husband, Ralph, and I developed a philosophy of opening our hearts by becoming foster parents.

Ralph came home for lunch one day as I was pulling our sixteen-month-old twins, Sean and Meghan, away from playing in the dishwasher. Out of the blue he asked, in a slow, matter-of-fact tone, "Do you think we should become foster parents?"

Even though at the time we had six young children, and three older ones, I did not hesitate. "Sure," I responded. It seemed a natural choice for us. Ralph and I had met through our work in special education: his in learning disabilities and mine in hearing impairment. I had always believed that children are one of God's greatest and most precious gifts.

I had first experienced this when I became a mom to my

three stepchildren, "my first teachers." It was Sarah, Hattie, and Zach who provided me with all of the joys and challenges of motherhood. Seasoned parents though we were—some might say middle-aged—our six birth children arrived in less than five years. Our oldest twins, Anne and Jane, were not yet five years old when our younger twins, Meghan and Sean, were born. In between were Matthew, age three, and Luke, fifteen months. It was a busy and happy time. We never completely lost our minds, although speaking in complete sentences became a thing of the past. Peace and harmony had given way to ordered chaos and lots of energy in our home.

In Ralph's work as director of special education, he was keenly aware that many children were deprived of love and security. Adding to our family pulled at our heartstrings, and so, with Ralph's fateful question, a new stage of our life began.

The decision to move ahead took a few minutes. The licensing, however, took a few months. Gradually, over the next several years, foster parenting became our life. When our first foster son arrived, we were elevated to sainthood among some and insanity among others. But our whole family agreed it was a blessing. Understanding that we were keeping kids safe, healthy, wanted, and happy (at least most of the time), overcame any frustration or worry.

With foster parenting, we came to the deep understanding that many of life's problems did not have quick solutions. I have often pondered the "children are only ours for a little while" bit of wisdom. I thought I understood it. Living it, however, was a painful process. Letting go of children whom you have grown to love is the hardest part. Trusting in God's unending love for his own children helped us through the pain.

Gifts flowed from the fostering experience. Our children developed deep compassion for others. And then God allowed us a gift beyond anything we had imagined: Two of our foster children became a permanent part of our family through adoption. When our youngest twins were seven, we prepared to adopt Casy, who was almost three, and Jimmy, just eighteen months.

Now my elderly parents needed help, and our family accepted the invitation to open our hearts even more. My parents had moved from New Hampshire to North Dakota where we lived when Sean and Meghan were three weeks old. Dad had progressive and debilitating arthritis, and Mom had been diagnosed with the beginning stages of Alzheimer's disease. Little tasks suddenly had become major obstacles for her, and Dad began living "the long good-bye" as he learned to let go of his beloved wife. They had a little house just blocks away from us. Eventually however, "nearby" was not close enough. Mom began falling and sometimes wandered through the neighborhood. Dad's progressive arthritis left him too weak to redirect her home.

The solution was clear: We needed to build an addition so my parents could live with us. Amid the chaos, blessings and fun emerged. There's nothing like sheetrock for kids to draw on, and with all the sawdust flying, I had a perfect excuse to take a break from dusting.

Ralph and I were convinced that our home would provide an engaging environment for Mom and a welcome relief for Dad. Indeed, both of them experienced a sense of peace as they let go of the worry and stress of living alone. Now, at age seventy-eight, Dad could read the paper, cook his famous spaghetti and meatballs, or take a nap in his chair—simple pleasures that had been taken from him.

For the next four months, Mom was fully engaged in life. While the kids played Grandma's favorite songs on their violins, she tapped her foot and smiled, and then asked them to play it again...and again. She loved to fold little towels, which she did so meticulously. What I would have finished in a snap became an afternoon's activity for Mom. Yet, even in her advanced stage of memory loss, Mom could tell the difference between helping me fold towels and the foolishness of stacking blocks for the occupational therapist. "Who does she think I am—a little kid?" she whispered to me. Watching the children simplify difficult tasks for their grandmother was a blessing. Speed and accuracy no longer mattered. Mom was getting the best occupational therapy in the world by doing meaningful work, and working with her grandchildren didn't seem burdensome to her. She was simply enjoying life with them.

In the midst of all this, foster parenting continued. Rocking and feeding our three-month-old foster baby was a source of peace for Mom. She could never be left alone with the baby, but wrapping her fingers around his little hand, she would whisper, "I don't know who you are, or where you came from, but you sure are cute. God love you." The stress paled in comparison to the joy that we shared with each other.

Joy aside, though, it was still a balancing act, but my dad had a way of driving home important lessons. When I lost one of the kids in the neighborhood, he reminded me of the agony in Mary's heart when Jesus was lost in the temple. I appreciated his holy slant, although I pointed out that the lost one wasn't in any temple doing anything of importance. Dad remained undeterred. "Just give them to God, honey. He will take care of them." We found the lost child shortly afterward.

Although I appeared to be a picture of competence, it was "in my weakness that his power was made perfect." There were times I grew anxious and worried, begging God for more compassion, more physical strength, more sleep. There were moments when my guilt about caring more for my parents than for my eight children caused me to drop to my knees, and I learned to fall more easily into God's protective arms.

The week before Christmas, Mom died, much like she had lived—quietly, peacefully, holding Dad's hand. Until then, death had been only a vague idea for the children. They felt that Grandma had died too soon.

Grandpa carried on without the love of his life. He spent more time in his chair and more time in prayer. His arthritis worsened. In quiet moments, we could hear him pray under his breath, "Just a little share in your Passion, Lord," as he rubbed his hands and knees to try and lessen the pain. With his head and body bent to his knees, he prayed continually for all of us.

Without any explanation from Ralph or me, the kids instinctively knew how to respond with attention to Grandpa, and the months following Mom's death, although difficult, overflowed with blessings. Sunday dinner with just Grandpa included ice cream for dessert. I did the dishes while Ralph and the kids listened to my dad tell stories of his youth. Whether it was the ice cream, a night off from washing dishes, or listening to Grandpa, it didn't matter. It was exactly what we all needed.

One by one, the children took on their new role in Grandpa's life: cooking for him, eating with him, and watching TV with him in the evenings after homework. Sean and Jimmy walked with him outside, one shuffled step at a time, their little hands on Grandpa's walker to guide him. He taught them new prayers. They bought him cans of peanuts, and then sat beside him, waiting for an offer to help themselves. An artist himself, Grandpa often guided young hands in art projects and taught them perspective in their sketches. He delighted in cups of coffee with just the right balance of cream and sugar, and the fight was on to see who could provide the best for him.

As time passed and his pain increased, Dad's mind began to fail. No doubt, God surrounded our house with all his holy angels on more than one occasion. Fire alarms going off in the kitchen became more frequent. There were days when I returned home after driving the children to school to find Dad calling my name at the top of the steps to our house, inches from going over the edge in his wheelchair.

When I allow myself to think of how I could have done things differently, one episode in particular comes to mind. The children had taken forever to settle down for the night. Three or four were sick and the youngest had gotten his foot stuck in the crib earlier. It had been a tough evening. At 1:30 in the morning, with the last load of laundry in the dryer and enough socks matched so as to not embarrass the oldest children in school the next day, I heard my dad's voice from his bedroom. "Kathleeeeeen!" he called, still with a trace of strength and authority. Running through the house, my heart beating uncontrollably, I was at his bedside in seconds.

Dad was propped up on his pillow, holding the crucifix that he slept with every night. Immediately realizing he wasn't hurt or in danger, I calmed down. Totally exhausted, I leaned against the bedroom door, my eyes barely open. He looked at me with great intent—the look only a father can give his little girl at any age.

"Kathy," he began. "Have you thought about how much Christ suffered in his Passion?" Not waiting for an answer, he continued. "Do you have any idea how much Christ suffered on the cross? Honey, do you ever think about the pain that our Blessed Mother must have felt watching her Son die?" As he spoke, tears filled his eyes. "Can you imagine?" He repeated, this time, to himself, "Can you imagine?"

I wish that I could recall this moment with great pride at how I allowed Dad's words to encourage my tired little soul. I did not. I stared at Dad in disbelief, not that he was so inspired and prayerful, but that he was still awake and I was completely exhausted. Politely, I responded "No, Dad. I guess I never thought of it just like that. Could we think about it together tomorrow? I'm really tired, Dad."

I kissed Dad goodnight, for the third or fourth time, and fell asleep on his couch. It was later that next day that I fully realized the missed opportunity. Dad lived for opportunities to do things for the love of God. He embraced human suffering, asking Christ daily for "just a little share in your passion." Dad had simply wanted to share this love and insight with me.

I believe God allows the precious moments in our lives to be forever imprinted in our minds. The hours before my father's death are one of those treasured memories. One by one, each child had time alone with Grandpa. One by one, they held his hand, kissed his cheek, swabbed his mouth with wet sponges, and prayed. No one really said much except to tell him over and over, "I love you." All his life, Dad had prayed to St. Joseph for a happy death. His prayers were answered with his children and grandchildren at his bedside, along with our priest, the rosary, and the litany of the saints. As we tearfully said good-bye to the man who had taught us about the most important things in life, we let go of a dad and a grandpa who changed us all in a profound way.

Today, when our children reminisce about the struggles and turmoil of those seven years with their grandparents, they have a sense of gratitude. They remember how they watched Grandpa recommit himself daily to living out his wedding vow "in sickness and in health, until death do us part." They learned not to rush through things—how even the most insignificant and simplest of tasks should be done with love. They discovered that joy could be found in small things. They also learned the meaning of self-sacrifice by watching Grandpa take care of Grandma when he could barely walk himself. Perhaps most importantly, they feel that they were given a "window" into the value of suffering and the true meaning of the Scripture passage, "Take up your cross and follow me."

Shortly after my father's death, a baby girl in need of foster care helped to fill the space in our hearts. Leah was eight days old when she was placed in our home. She is now six years old and, through adoption, is now our youngest daughter. God continues to fill our home with love.

THE MOST SUCCESSFUL WOMAN IN THE WORLD

Stacy Trasancos

WHY ON EARTH do I do this? I screamed to myself as I stood in the middle of the kitchen, which had just exploded. All was calm when I walked out of it a minute ago, but now Cocoa Puffs and spilt milk were everywhere. Two daughters were in a screaming armlock; the other two were missing in action. My toddler waddled in his sagging diaper across the kitchen and reached up to me, whining. He wanted to nurse—again.

I tried to pray for patience as I surveyed the disaster, but it was too late. I was already screeching like a deranged heathen for some peace and order in the household.

Why did I pick this life? And why can't I handle it? Nights in a house with five little kids are full of ups and downs, which only leaves me lying awake in anxiety about our two older ones who are no longer living under the protection of this roof. The drama hits in waves throughout the day, and sometimes it's overwhelming.

That morning, upon surveying the complete mess in the kitchen, I did what I often do after losing control of myself like this: I courageously retreated to the bathroom to hide. *You fail-*

ure, I thought, staring at the image in the mirror. I cried and felt sorry for myself.

You would never have guessed by the scene that morning that I once drove a little convertible two-seater sports car, donned smart business attire and perfectly coiffed my hair each day. You would never believe I once walked through my own research lab, where white-coated technicians did exactly as I instructed them in an orderly, precise, and immaculate fashion. I would then settle into a quiet and tidy office to work on complex problems that affected one of the largest industries in the world: clothing. I had left my career as a senior research chemist for DuPont Lycra® to navigate motherhood.

So why did I trade all this for motherhood? I don't like chaos, I don't like to be messy, I don't like to be out of control, and I never thought babies smelled good. As my emotional reaction to the kitchen frenzy subsided I remembered why.

When my husband and I got married, I thought being successful was what men wanted. Tall? Check. Thin? Check. Blonde hair and blue eyes? Check. Check. Appearance put together to a 't'? Check. Accomplished? You'd better believe it. The truth is, the man married a snob, a self-centered, "have-it-all" show-off. I had been so busy trying to appear perfect that I never really considered what my husband actually wanted.

I recalled those faraway days early in our marriage when I had found out I was pregnant. I had freaked out, and my frightened husband was introduced to the head-spinning monster that could overcome his new wife. I was mad at him and at myself. After weeks of coming-to-term-with-pregnancy melt-downs over the injustice of it all, my husband addressed me in a moment of clarity:

"Stacy," he finally said, "How do you define success?"

"I've worked hard to get where I am," I answered. "I want a nice house and nice cars, I want to look good and be healthy, I don't want to gain a hundred pounds and suffer through pregnancy. I want to rise up that career ladder and make a name for myself. I want to publish and retire well-known." *I want, I want, I want* echoed in my head.

My husband was persistent but treaded lightly. "At the end of your life," his strong, gentle voice continued, "will those things have made you successful?"

The question shook me up. I had barely acknowledged, much less made sense of, the emptiness I felt inside, even as I was living society's definition of success. My metrics for achievement were all external; they depended on how I measured up to other people's standards. Suddenly, I saw how continuing that hollow existence for the rest of my life would result in an empty claim to success. I know it sounds cliché, but the image of "Successful, Blonde, Well-Dressed Scientist and Homeowner" on my gravestone suddenly seemed, well, shallow.

There was another painful reality. As an off-and-on single mother, I had been absent much of the time during my older two children's childhood. Oh, I'd gone through the motions—feeding them, dressing them, taking them to school—but I hadn't been much of a real mother to them.

When my husband promised me that he would take care of the family if I wanted to stay home with the new baby, a little flicker ignited within me. He would be a father and a husband who provides, if I would let him. After six months, I decided to stay home. I also decided to be open to life.

The perfectionist in me decided that if I were going to stay home and raise children, then, by golly, I'd better have a bunch of them. My decision to be open to life wasn't exactly a virtuous one, but God has his mysterious ways of meeting people where they are and guiding them. Just before our second daughter was born, I found myself enrolled in R.C.I.A. classes, and I slowly began a long process of conversion. I wanted our children to grow up in church, and my husband suggested the Catholic Church. My decision to be Catholic was no more intellectual than that, but little by little my eyes and heart were opened, and I began to thirst for truth.

When our third daughter was baptized, I was also confirmed, and my husband and I celebrated our sacramental marriage that same weekend. Since then we have welcomed another daughter and a son into our family, and we're still ready to welcome more, even with our aging bodies.

I've learned along the way that success is hard and evasive. It doesn't automatically come through wearing smart and stylish clothes in the laboratory or casual wear in the kitchen. Success takes a lot of hard work, and no family is perfect. I no longer live in fear of rejection, however. I've become a strong woman, the kind of woman who can confront problems and not let it break her, a woman whose strength and beauty isn't dependent on external metrics decided by other people. My metrics are internal, a conversation in my soul with God. I strive for virtue because I know that when I do, graces are abundant.

Leading souls to heaven, a mother's top priority, always imposes the duty of suffering. That's what brings me closer to Christ and infuses me with strength. I lift my eyes trustfully to heaven and offer my sorrows to the One who will reward me abundantly with graces. My husband and I frequent the sacraments, pray together, and refuse to ever give up.

So, concluding my little reprieve in the bathroom, I remembered that question, "How do you define success?" I stood up, squared my shoulders, and faced the mirror again. Perfect or not, I was going to get through another day, with God's help.

I prayed my usual prayer for protection, made the sign of the cross, swept my arms wide, and kicked my slipper-clad foot high in the air, sending my tattered old robe flying. With that motion, I effectively kicked Satan and his lies out of my home.

As my hair fell out of the rubber band holding it on top of my head and landed around my shoulders, I even slung it back triumphantly as I repeated my prayer for protection again. I prayed for enough grace to restore the kitchen to an acceptable tidiness and, breathing in a renewed determination, I wiped my eyes, opened the door, and was immediately overtaken with big eyes staring up at me. I saw little mouths quick with apologies and declarations of love, as tiny, sticky arms of affection were thrown around my neck. Soon, I was laughing. And so were my children.

Now, *that's* success.

SIGNS ALONG THE WAY

Frank Russo

IT WAS THE spring of 1979. I was a Division Manager at AT&T and the proud father of six children ages two through eleven. Four of the kids were in grade school, and I was beginning to think about how much Catholic high school would cost. Then, in early May, my wife Bette told me we might be having a seventh child.

I'm ashamed to say I was not happy to hear that. I started to think about how this was going to affect my retirement plans—I would probably have to work until I was ninety years old to pay the college bills alone. Our four-bedroom house was really getting crowded. I worried about Bette going through the difficulties of pregnancy at age thirty-five, with her varicose veins. Having another child with six others so young was going to be really tough.

On top of all this, for a number of years I had been experiencing doubts about my faith. Did God really exist? Was Jesus really his Son? Was there really a heaven and a hell? The Christian message is truly an incredible one: that there is a supernatural being we call God who created the world and the entire universe, who knows exactly what each of us is going to do today and tomorrow, and who loves us very much. Even more difficult to believe, I thought, was that this God would send his own Son to suffer and die for us and then be raised from the dead.

On the one hand I wanted very much to believe these things, and I felt it was not absurd to do so. But on the other hand, there were thousands of brilliant scientists, philosophers, and educators who placed no credence in any of these truths. After all, I was Catholic primarily because my parents were.

So, faced with these two "problems" of a seventh child and my growing doubts about God, what did I do? Well, after work one day I went to St. Peter's Church in downtown Manhattan, the oldest Catholic Church in the state of New York. I pleaded with God to help me with these two "problems."

"God, if you are there, I am sorry but I do not want a seventh child," I prayed. "Haven't I done my fair share with six kids? So many others are only having two or three." I then asked God to show me he truly existed by not giving us this seventh child, and by doing it in a way that would be a very clear sign to me.

"Please make it so clear, Lord, that it's like hitting me over the head with a bat," I told him. I had no idea how he would do this, but I knew if God existed then he could find a way.

At that moment, an idea occurred to me as I looked at the clock in the church. It read 5:15. So I added, "And please do it in a way that clearly has something to do with 5:15."

I went home actually thinking that maybe Bette had discovered, precisely at 5:15, that she wasn't pregnant after all. That did not happen. "Well, then," I surmised, "maybe it will be at 5:15 AM." The next morning, if you can believe this, I woke Bette shortly after 5:15 to ask her if she still thought she was pregnant. She was not happy to be awakened that early to be asked such a dumb question. "You woke me to ask me that?"

A couple of days later Bette went to the doctor and learned that she was indeed pregnant. I was dismayed—retirement was now pushed back to age ninety, we would have a more crowded house, and Bette would have to go through another pregnancy. But worse still, in my mind, was the fact that God had failed to respond to my heartfelt request to strengthen my faith by giving me this sign.

I was not a happy camper. But practical person that I am, I focused on the "problem" at hand. To help Bette with her varicose vein problem, I suggested that perhaps she ought to jog around our local pond in order to minimize the effects of the pregnancy on her veins. She checked with the doctor who said it would be fine. Bette jogged the next morning…but it was not fine. Some problems developed as a result of the jogging. She went back to a second doctor who said that jogging was a mistake. The pregnancy was now in trouble—big trouble! I figured if there were a God, he was now going to punish me for my selfish attitude. For the next two months Bette and I worried about her pregnancy. Would the baby live? Would he be normal and healthy? Then on Friday, July 6th, 1979, at 1:45 PM, Bette had a miscarriage. I called our pastor and the doctor, who told us to go to the hospital. By the time Bette was admitted it was past three o'clock.

The timing of this miscarriage could not have been worse. The following day, we were in charge of hosting a large picnic with all of Bette's Irish cousins and their families, well over a hundred people. I had to leave Bette in the hospital to gather some of the kids, get them dinner, and prepare for the picnic the next day. I took our four oldest to a fast-food restaurant. I recall standing in line to place my order and looking at the clock: It read 5:15. I thought, "This is not what I meant when I asked God to not burden me with a seventh child. I meant for Bette not to be pregnant. I never wanted her to have a miscarriage!"

Be that as it may, what happened was clearly not an answer to my prayer because this had nothing at all to do with 5:15. I was saddened at the miscarriage, ashamed of my very selfish attitude, but most of all disappointed that my serious request for a sign from God went completely unanswered.

When I got back home, my mother-in-law told me that I had to get back to the hospital because a major problem had developed. I hurried to the hospital and went to Bette's room. She had IV tubes in her arms.

"What happened?" I asked.

"Love, you never should've left me," she said weakly. "No one ever came to check on me. I was left in bed bleeding for all those hours since the miscarriage." The hospital had a great reputation, and so I was surprised to hear this.

"I felt myself getting weaker and weaker...I was about to pass out from the loss of blood. I tried to push the call button, but I didn't even have the strength to do that," Bette continued. "Thank goodness the woman in the bed next to me saw that I was in trouble and called for the nurse." I was dumbfounded that something like this could happen at such a prestigious hospital. "The nurse came in," said Bette, "and couldn't get a good pulse or blood pressure reading. She called the resident who called for the attending physician, who then ordered the IVs."

Somewhat in a state of shock, I automatically asked Bette, "When did all this happen?" expecting her to say something like, "Right after you left me," or "A little while ago." Instead she answered, "It happened at 5:15." I sat down on her bed and began to cry. How could I have prayed such a selfish prayer?

Still hanging onto some skepticism, I asked her how she knew it was 5:15, since there was no clock in the room and Bette wasn't wearing a watch. "I don't know," she said. She had no idea why I was pushing for this explanation. I asked her again, "Were you just guessing?"

"What's the big deal?" she wanted to know.

I told her it was very important for me to know. She thought some more and then recalled that the doctor asked the nurse, "What time is it?" and the nurse answered, "5:15."

I interpreted this message from God as taking me by the scruff of the neck, and saying "Frank, you big dummy, you were so worried about the burden of a seventh child...well, compare that to losing your wife!" I have thought about my selfish attitude on many occasions since then, often asking the child that we lost to please forgive me. Indeed, I do that even to this day. For several months I told relatives and friends this story of how God answered—in his own way—that request of mine two months earlier. But guess what? After a few months, I began wondering if I wasn't blowing this thing out of proportion. Perhaps this was all one big coincidence, I thought. I was still skeptical.

The next part of this story begins in the early summer of 1981. I was in Florida on AT&T business. I called Bette that night to check in on things and learned that she lost the diamond from her engagement ring, which she had known was loose in its setting. All I cared about was the financial loss, not any sentimental loss. "No insurance," I thought, "and not high enough for a casualty tax deduction." Oh, was I upset. "Get the kids and conduct an organized search, and if that fails, pray to St. Anthony," I said. The more I thought about it, the angrier I got. "How could Bette have been so careless?"

That night I got on my knees in my hotel room. "Lord, I am not playing any games here. I honestly don't know if that hospital near-death scene at 5:15 was your answer to my prayer or not. It sure looked like it was, but in all honesty, I am not really positive. Could we please do this again, Lord? Would you give me a sign of your existence and show me that Jesus is indeed your risen Son by helping us find that lost diamond?" It was midnight, so I added, "And could finding the diamond have something to do with 12:00?"

The next day I called home and was hoping to hear that the diamond had been found at noon. No such luck. I called the next afternoon again, but still nothing.

Returning home from that business trip, I arranged for Bette to pick me up at La Guardia airport. Bette was right on time, and we drove home together. I was focused on that lost diamond and wondering why Bette, who knew it was loose, had not been more careful. It seemed to make me feel better by blaming her for losing it. Clearly, this was not a good way to think or behave.

As we neared home, Bette asked me to stop at a store. While I waited for her, I wondered if she might have been driving when the stone fell out. I got out of the car and began looking on the floor in front of the driver's seat, which was largely covered with beach sand. All of a sudden, I spotted the diamond shining in the sand! I picked it up and ran into the store to show Bette. But it was not twelve noon, nor midnight, and so this couldn't have been an answer to my prayer for a sign from God.

The next day as I sat in our family room watching some boxing matches on TV, I kept wondering why God would possibly answer my first prayer but not my second. Yes, we found the diamond, and I was very happy about that, but I had clearly specified the time to be 12 o'clock. Then I started thinking about the exact timing of my finding of the diamond. As I thought about it and calculated the distances and times, I suddenly realized that we must have found the diamond precisely at 5:15. God had answered my prayer after all!

As I thought about it, it seemed God was reminding me that he was in charge, and so I was not free to play games by willy-nilly picking this time or that, choosing the terms of the agreement, and thereby "testing" him. It was remarkable enough to find that small diamond—but finding it at 5:15 was, in my mind, sending me a two-part message: one part answered my request and the other reminded me that I am NOT in charge—he is!

Again, for several months I told relatives and friends of this "miracle sign," but again after a few months I began to wonder if I wasn't blowing this out of proportion. Part of me was strongly inclined to believe, but the skeptical part was still uncertain.

The final part of this story begins in January of 1982 when I learned that, with the breakup of the Bell System, I was going to have to move to New Jersey and work for an affiliated company, Bell Communications Research. It seemed to be a very uncertain and undesirable situation—both the job and the move to New Jersey.

So for one last time in 1983 I went to St. Peter's Church and prayed to God, asking for one final miracle and one final sign: a division-level position with New York Telephone. This would enable me to work at a comparable job level without having to move my family. I promised God that, should he grant me this,

I would never ever doubt again and I would ask for no more signs. "Lord, I recognize your message to me last time," I said, "and so we'll stick with a sign that has something to do with the number 5-15. And please make it a very clear sign." I was hoping that he would grant me this request of a division-level job at New York Telephone on May 15th (5-15). I also agreed to go to Mass every day for thirty days, which for me was a big sacrifice.

To my dismay, May 15th came and went with nothing remotely promising on the horizon with New York Telephone. By January of the following year, things were looking very bleak. We began looking at houses in New Jersey, and even found one across from Drew University in Madison. We also began the process of putting our home on the market.

I remember that Bette and I held one of our semiannual family conferences that February. We held these family conferences every six months to hear from our kids as a group: what was on their minds, what problems were they having with friends, with school, with us their parents.

At this February conference I told the family that I was unable to get a good job with New York Telephone and that we'd have to relocate to New Jersey.

My daughter Liz piped up, "But Dad, aren't you at least going to wait until May 15th?" I was stunned. I didn't even know she knew about my 5-15 prayer requests over the past five years.

"Liz, how do you know about this?" I asked. "I heard you talking about it to Uncle Andy," she said.

I was disheartened because I knew there was no chance of

getting out of this relocation as I had been trying without success to get a position for well over a year.

"Liz," I explained, "it's just not possible. For some reason God must want us to move to New Jersey," I said. Then Liz said something I'll never forget. "Dad," she said, "you have no faith!"

I couldn't believe what she said. Part of me was thinking that this squirt of a fifteen-year-old kid was just too naïve to understand the complexities of modern day business and the realities of life. But another part of me was truly touched by Liz's own deep faith.

"No," I said, "Liz, we are going to have to move and that's it."

Those months, from the fall of 1982 until February of 1984 were, without a doubt, the worst period of my life. I was so depressed I would often go to bed by 8:00 each night, even after the kids' birthday parties. On top of all this, my best friend, Bob, was very sick. As it turned out, he had AIDS and was dying. He was the godfather of our daughter Liz. We were unaware of his hidden life until we learned he had AIDS. All his friends had deserted him, but Bette and I remained close to him until the end. Bette, saint that she is, even offered Bob the possibility to live his final months with our family. At the time, it was not exactly clear how AIDS was spread, so Bob was advised by his doctor not to accept our offer. But he was moved by her generosity and told me later that he was offering all his terrible suffering—and it was indeed terrible—for my special prayer request.

During this time, I went to lunch with Harvey Walton, a fellow manager at AT&T and a devout evangelical Christian. I told him of my request for a sign and the story of my first two requests, which seemed granted. Harvey then told me I sounded like Gideon in the Book of Judges. He related that Gideon was about to go into battle with an enemy of Israel, but he was fearful. He asked God for a sign that he should indeed go into battle at that time. He got the sign, but then just like me, Gideon began to doubt. And so, he asked for a second sign. And again, God answered him, giving him the confidence to go into battle, which he of course won.

"But," said Harvey, "Gideon only did it twice. You are asking for a third sign, Frank, and that may be going too far." I was taken aback by the story of Gideon. That evening, I checked the story in my own Bible. But I was thrilled to learn that Gideon had actually made three requests for signs! Knowing this made me hopeful about my own third request.

In March, an opportunity for a position with New York Telephone suddenly appeared. I thought I had a good shot at it, so we slowed down the moving process. But on Good Friday I was deeply disappointed to learn that plans had changed and the position was eliminated. The following week, though, another position suddenly opened up. Negotiations proceeded slowly, but in the right direction. I remember the weekend of May 12th and 13th. I was increasingly convinced I would get the job, and all I now wanted to know was *when* I would officially be told I have it. My four oldest children were now aware of all this, which accentuated the significance of the date. Finally, on Tuesday morning, *May 15th*, my boss called me to tell me I had the job!

In all honesty, I was far more excited over the date than the fact that I had gotten the job! I remember walking home that evening and seeing my son Terence, age eleven, riding his bicycle. When he spotted me he yelled out, "Dad, did you get the job today?"

From that day on, my priorities and, indeed, my life were forever changed. Money and concern over retirement went from the top of my list to the bottom. Never again would I doubt the existence of God, or that Jesus died for us and rose from the dead. Never again would I question the teachings of the Church. It was the beginning of a commitment to work for others rather than for myself. I believe that the prayers and sufferings of my friend Bob played an important role in bringing this about.

From that day onward, I kept my promise and never again asked God for any more signs. But as if not to be outdone in generosity, God continued to send me signs of his presence, especially in troubled times. In particular, there are three separate occasions when he has sent me a gentle "5-15" reminder. All three of them involve my daughter Liz and her husband Kent.

When Liz became engaged to Kent Kilges in 1990, Bette and I were concerned that he was a non-practicing, non-church-going Protestant of sorts, who held a largely secular and agnostic worldview. He seemed to have the human virtues, but we were concerned that his non-Christian worldview would pose serious problems for their marriage in the future. We made our concerns known to Liz, who let us know that it was a major concern for her as well.

Liz's wedding on June 21, 1991, at St. Peter's Church was beautiful. A month or so after the wedding I was looking at the 400 proofs taken by the photographer. I was anxious to see the ones showing me walking Liz down the aisle, which, for most fathers of daughters, is the highlight of the wedding—at least it was for me. As I looked at the pictures, I suddenly noticed one that included the bottom two-thirds of the clock in the rear of the church. I couldn't believe what I was seeing: The clock read "5:15." From that moment on, I've never worried about that marriage.

But this doesn't mean that we ever stopped praying for Kent's conversion. In fact, Liz would often tell God that she would suffer anything to achieve Kent's conversion. She has since told us that the "anything" she was imagining were such terrible things as "gaining a lot of weight" or "developing acne." She had no idea of the suffering that was right around the corner for her and Kent.

Kent and Liz's daughter Elie was born on September 3rd, 1993, and died in 2004 at age ten as a result of a brain tumor that was operated on, unsuccessfully, when she was nine months old. Kent is a brilliant writer and has written a book about his daughter called *A Grace Given* (published by Scepter Publishers). In one chapter, Kent writes about his thoughts one evening in March of 1994 when Elie was seven months old and they thought she was perfectly healthy.

One evening, I sat in the rocking chair, staring out the window of our living room. The night was black. There was no moon, but the sky was full of stars. I had been thinking all evening about religion and Catholicism. It struck me how important it was for Liz. Perhaps I should be open to the possibility of religious feeling in spite of my lack of inclination. I decided to leave it up to God, and so I prayed, "God, if it is your will that I become a Catholic, if Christ has some relevance to me, and if religion is something that I should embrace, give me some kind of sign." I stood and moved to the window, half-expecting a shooting star or some other dramatic event. I watched intently. Nothing happened. Then Liz called—she needed a diaper to change Elie. How silly I was being, I thought. Soon I forgot my request of God. It was easy to forget my prayer when nothing happened. One month later we found out Elie would die from a brain tumor.

The doctors initially told Liz and Kent the tumor was inoperable, but their hopes were brightened when they discovered a specialist who thought he could save Elie. At the time, I remember wondering whether Elie's terrible affliction was in some way linked to Kent's spiritual growth and possible conversion. When Elie went into surgery on, of all days, May 15th, 1994, my conviction grew that this terrible situation was possibly related to Liz's prayer for Kent's conversion. This date was exactly ten years to the day after the third and final sign God kindly gave me on May 15th, 1984.

While the operation saved Elie's life, she unfortunately suffered a stroke in the recovery room and became bedridden at home for the next ten years. She was blind and never able to talk or walk or even turn in her bed. Liz and Kent took loving care of Elie for all those years, and now their daughter is, I feel certain, a saint in heaven.

Kent has written his book about Elie in a far, far more spiritual manner than I would have ever dreamed possible back at their engagement in 1990. It is a beautifully written book, with great comments by George Weigel, author of Pope John Paul II's official biography, and a great introduction by Father Bob Connor, a priest of Opus Dei. This book is a sort of culmination of Elie's lifelong impact on Kent, and for that matter, on many others.

The final sign from God that reassured me about Liz and Kent's marriage actually involved this book. *A Grace Given* was completed in late 2007 and self-published via Barnes & Noble and Amazon.com in the late winter of 2007-08. When Liz went to pick up the first thousand copies of the book from the printer in upstate New York, she called me and said, "Dad, I'm at the printer, and you're not going to believe this—what do you think the address is? It's 515 Lee Street." A coincidence? I don't think so. For me, this was a sign from God showing me that Liz' early prayers for Kent, followed by Elie's illness, and Kent's spiritual odyssey are all somehow tied together. On Pentecost Sunday, 2009, Kent was received into the Catholic Church.

From that first prayer at 5:15 PM in St. Peter's Church to this final sign at 515 Lee Street in upstate New York, God has made his presence felt in my life. It wasn't an easy process, but I eventually came to see that God is real, that he is close to me, and that I can trust him in everything. I no longer need signs along the way.

GROWING UP BIG HEARTED

Theresa Kloska Thomas

THE DIGITAL CLOCK in the kitchen reads 7:40 A.M., but it's really 7:10. The clock has been set ahead by a half hour to get everyone moving on the time. Three pajama-clad and giggling preschoolers slide backward down the stairs and race into the family room to turn on cartoons. Mom is sitting on a recliner there, feeding the baby and sipping a cup of steaming coffee.

"Morning, guys," she says, and smiles as another child slips behind a rocker to spy on them. Suddenly, her husband and seventeen-year-old son rush through the room, the latter with half a donut hanging from his mouth as he slips his jacket on.

"Be back around noon," Dad explains, lightly kissing Mom's cheek. He grabs his golf clubs and is gone. Mom sets the baby down on a blanket and pads into the kitchen for a coffee refill. Her ten-, eleven-, and twelve-year-olds are clanging dishes and banging cupboards, finding their own breakfasts.

"Hey, look!" yells Mike, the eleven-year-old. "Mom bought Lucky Charms!"

"No way!" shouts ten-year-old Jeff, and immediately the others rush to the cereal cupboard.

"I get it second!"

"Hey, leave some for the rest of us!"

"There's plenty for all of you," says Mom calmly, producing another box of the popular cereal. As she reaches for the coffeepot, she spots several notes scribbled on napkins from her older daughters:

> *Lisa up at 8:00. Volleyball workouts at 10. Please get*
> *Cheryl and Karen up to do aerobics at 7:30.*

This was a typical Saturday morning in my home when I was growing up, where there were thirteen kids, including one foster child, ranging in age from six months to twenty-two years. Others often speculated about our family. "She (Mom) must run that house like an army camp"; "I wonder what their grocery bill is like"; and "They must always be washing clothes!" are just some of the comments I routinely heard. For the record, Mom didn't run the house like an army, although meals were often cafeteria style. Mom and Dad's monthly grocery bill was always high, as they valued good nutrition. At one point they figured they went through 1,176 napkins, thirty-one loaves of bread and ninety gallons of milk a month!

At home with thirteen children, the washing machine was always running. In fact, it was a family joke that we didn't merely categorize dirty clothes into "darks," "lights," and "brights," but individual loads of "navy blues," "light blues," "royal blues," "yellows," "oranges," "greens," and "reds." We were just an average family of four—times three-and-a-half! To many, such a large family seemed impractical, but my parents liked impractical things—like getting married when they were both twenty-one and still in school.

Mom, who came from a family of three children, worked full-time at the telephone company selling phone equipment to businesses. Dad, who came from a family of five children, attended Aquinas College in Grand Rapids, Michigan, played golf with the college team (he was on an athletic scholarship and that was the only way for him to bridge the gap between the money he had and tuition) and worked full-time at the post office at night. Dad had barely enough time to devote to school and work and no extra money, yet my parents—with great hope and faith—became engaged. After a Polish wedding in the Basilica and a reception in a hall with mostly family, they settled into a tiny apartment.

One summer evening, when they were at a fair, my father won a silver ID bracelet for my mother by tossing rings around the necks of Coke bottles. When the fair attendant asked Dad what he wanted engraved on the cheap silver jewelry, he replied evenly, "Fourteen or bust."

"Mind if I ask fourteen what?" the attendant asked.

Dad says he looked at Mom, and Mom answered. "Kids," she said.

Even then, my parents were determined to have an impractically large family. Nine months and nine days after wedding, their family began with a baby girl: Me. Eleven months later came my sister Cheryl, then in succession Karen, Bobby, Lisa, Jenny, Mike, Jeff, Mary, BJ, Kathy, and Joey. Mom suffered a miscarriage after Joey and was not able to get pregnant again. After surgery for varicose veins, Mom suggested another impractical thing to Dad: becoming foster parents.

Mom always loved babies, and when she couldn't have any more of her own, she missed them. She missed them so much that when she saw a notice in our church bulletin asking for foster families to keep infants until they could be placed with adoptive families, she pulled Dad aside.

"Couldn't we do this?" she asked, "just for awhile?" Dad's financial situation had come a long way since his post office days, and by then he was the owner of a flourishing hardwood dimension mill. My parents were by no means rich, but Dad was doing well and with just a bit of sacrifice, Mom knew they could afford to take in another child.

"Please? We have enough room, and besides," she continued, tapping the bulletin lightly with her index finger, "this says it would only be for a few weeks."

At first, Dad seemed skeptical. "Don't you have enough to do?" he asked her. There were soccer and baseball games, golf and music lessons for the younger kids already, not to mention the hectic work and practice schedules of the older ones. With a baby, Dad pointed out, Mom would be much less free to take the children to their activities. And of course there would be more laundry. And what about when the babies eventually left?

Would it be difficult for the family to adjust? How would they explain what was happening to a three-year-old? Would it be worth all the trouble when we wouldn't even have the reward of seeing the foster children grow up?

Mom and Dad disappeared into the living room. When they emerged an hour later, they called us all together and told us what they had in mind. Our large family would grow larger.

Before our family could start receiving infants into the home, my parents had to become licensed by the state. Social workers had to interview Mom and Dad, a fire marshal came to inspect our home, and Mom and Dad had to fill out forms and submit themselves for evaluation. Once the official procedure was complete, there was the long wait for the state to process the application.

Mom and Dad finally received the license to care for two foster children at a time, and in September 1983 a baby named Nathan came to live with us. He was a cute little fellow with a tuft of light fuzzy hair on the top of his head. He had lively blue eyes that peeked out from behind chubby pink cheeks, and we immediately fell in love with him.

The social worker whisked Nathan away to adoptive parents after a few short weeks, leaving behind fourteen people who would never be the same again.

Growing up in a big family—a big-hearted family—was adventuresome and wonderful. So wonderful, in fact, I couldn't wait to replicate the fun and surprises by having a large family of my own. While the size of the American family is shrinking, I'm happy to share that blessings from the Lord are in no short supply over here. My husband and I are raising nine of our own. My family of origin may have been a "family like no other," but the new family we've created is also unique. Yours is, too!

ONE WAITING FOR US

Patti Maguire Armstrong

"HEY, MARK, WE'RE going to have another baby," I announced
to my husband. We looked at each other, wide-eyed. We had
recently added an orphan boy from Kenya, so we were already
a family of eleven. We shared a strong understanding that each
little soul is a gift from God that will last an eternity. Still, I'd be
forty-seven and Mark forty-eight when this baby was due.

As we adjusted to the news, I discovered that our willingness
to accept new life led us closer to God. Instead of thinking of
things like money, the opinions of others, and our advanced age,
we decided to trust God to provide for us in this transitory world.
New life had begun and would forever be a part of our family.

Just the previous week, my eight-year-old daughter, Teresa,
had expressed hope that I would have another baby. When I
pointed out that older women did not usually have babies, she
reminded me that Elizabeth was older when she had John the
Baptist. I just smiled and said, "You never know."

Well, now we knew. The younger kids were ecstatic. I
thought the older kids would be taken aback (we had one in col-

lege, three in high school, one in junior high, and four younger ones), but they all said that given my history, they pretty much expected it. Friends and family registered surprise. After all, they had been secretly guessing that we were finally "done."

Then, at three months, I miscarried for the first time. I had some early warnings, so by the time it happened, it was not a surprise. The enormity of my loss did not really hit me until I was alone at morning Mass a couple of days later. I had requested that my kids ask God to let us know the sex of the baby. My oldest, Aaron, suggested I give it a unisex name and leave it at that. "I would really like to know who it was," I explained, "so please ask God to somehow let us know."

It was just before Mass, two days after the miscarriage, that I suddenly felt a deep sense of knowing that the baby had been a boy—Matthew. We chose that name to go with our Mark, Luke, and John members of the family. Realizing I had a son suddenly filled me with a deep awareness that my very own child was with God now. I knew there was no greater place to be, but still, a maternal sadness washed over me. My little son, Matthew, was our only baby I did not get to hold in my arms and have with me. He was the only one that his big brothers and sisters missed out on in this world.

I shed a few tears but was filled with peace that I knew who my baby was now. Then, after Mass, before leaving for home, the thought occurred to me that although I was convinced I had a son in heaven, other family members (especially the teens) might say, "Mom, you really don't know for sure."

I sent up a quick prayer. "Dear God, I accept that my son is with you now, but it would mean a lot to me if you would somehow let the others know the baby was a boy." I wanted my husband to know his son and my children to have a relationship with a little brother in heaven.

I kept the morning's experience to myself. Then, just a few hours later, Aaron called me from Fargo, where he attended college and was living for the summer. "Mom, I'm in a big hurry, but I just wanted to call to tell you I know the baby was a boy."

Aaron had dreamed two nights in a row of a baby. In the first dream, a baby had died but Aaron didn't know who he was. The next night, he had the same dream, but this time, when he looked at the baby, he knew it was his little brother. In the dream he looked at me, and we nodded at one another in understanding.

"Oh, Aaron, I just asked God this morning to somehow let everyone else know it was a boy." I explained my own experience to him, marveling at my answered prayer. My oldest had connected with my youngest, from earth to heaven.

There was no more time to talk, however, because Aaron was in a hurry to participate in a study, which paid very good money to college students. I learned the rest of the story later.

Aaron arrived at the study site only minutes after our conversation. By all rights, he should have been disqualified during the screening because his heart began racing when his pulse was taken. Since the study had been overbooked, they were looking for any reason to start bumping students, and Aaron knew from experience that an above-normal heart rate was a typical reason. It was Aaron's nervousness that caused his fast heart rate, but he could not get himself to calm down. He began asking his little brother, Matthew, to help him. His pulse was taken two more times, each time measuring faster than the previous rate.

It seemed hopeless. The study director looked at him and then at the nurse beside him who was recording the results. "Please, Matthew," Aaron prayed. "Please help me get into this study." He braced himself, waiting to be told he was dismissed. *There's no way now,* he thought.

Looking Aaron in the eyes, the director stated quietly to the nurse at his side: "Let him in." The nurse registered surprise. She opened her mouth as if to protest but then quickly followed the doctor as they went on to the next participant. A euphoric disbelief and awe filled Aaron's soul. It seemed impossible. He was in! And it was his little brother that got him in. It had to be.

It's been over eight years now since we lost Matthew, although, spiritually speaking, we will never lose him. He will always love us, his family, and always hear our prayers. He knows more than we do, and his love is greater than ours. Even though it would have been great to hold him on this earth, it is a grace to have him holding us in his heart now in heaven.

I WOULDN'T CHANGE A THING

Jeffery Gross

"CYS..CYSTIC...WHAT?" I asked the doctor. It was 1973, and my wife Connie and I had just been told that our nine-month-old son had a medical condition called cystic fibrosis. It was a lot for a young couple to learn. I could barely pronounce the word at the time.

Becoming a father was one of the most exciting moments in my life. I was out-of-this-world ecstatic. Dallas was born nine-and-a-half months after Connie and I married. Both of us were from farm families and married when I was twenty-one and Connie was eighteen. We couldn't wait to have a family of our own.

Connie went into labor in the middle of the night. At 10:21 AM, our blue-eyed, blonde-haired son was born. What a feeling it was to hold him in my arms! It was April 1, which meant that when I called our families, several of them thought it was an April Fools' joke. A couple of them even called the hospital to make sure I was really there.

Dallas was healthy at birth, but he always seemed to have a cold, and he struggled to gain weight. Every month, he slipped lower down on the growth charts, even though he had a good appetite and a happy disposition. After Connie joined me for a work conference and we left him with her mother for a couple days, we returned and saw our son through new eyes. "Something is not right," Connie insisted. I knew it, too.

We brought him in to the doctor. "He has cystic fibrosis (CF)," the doctor gently told us, and then added, "There is no cure."

All the time we thought Dallas just had a cold, we learned that it was his disease causing a thick, sticky build-up in his lungs. As we got the news, my first thought was, *We wanted to have a half a dozen kids; why us?* But Connie and I shared a strong faith in God. I had not been expecting this, but it did not take me long to ask, "Why not us?" I trusted God to pull us through.

The doctor explained that Dallas would need four breathing treatments a day, along with eleven different expensive medications. At that time, the expected life span of a child with CF was only around twenty.

Since CF was genetic, we were told that there was a 25 percent chance that any future baby of ours would also have the disease. Regardless, we never considered not having more children—not for an instant. Instead, Connie and I prayed and trusted God. We practiced Natural Family Planning to space our children so we could handle the extra care Dallas required.

The fact that our children might not live a long life had no bearing on our decision to have more babies. God puts us on this earth for a short time; it's not important how long we live but that we go to heaven one day. For me, a shorter life was not so hard to accept.

When Dallas was three, his little sister Taunia was born robust and healthy, with no sign of the disease. Caring for a new baby along with Dallas was a labor of love, but in addition new worries about Dallas emerged. Dallas did not walk until he was almost two, and even then, his coordination was poor. When Dallas was five, our doctor referred us to a neurologist. A muscle biopsy revealed that he had the worst kind of Muscular Dystrophy.

I am an optimist at heart. My philosophy is that whatever problem I have, I can look to my left or right and find someone who has it worse. This time, however, I had a hard time looking outside our family. I knew my family needed me to be strong, though. "God, give me the strength," I prayed.

We learned Dallas' muscles would deteriorate, and he would likely not live past his teens. The doctor also informed us that there was a 100 percent chance that any boy baby we had would have the same disease. "Well, Lord," I prayed, "You better give me girls, then." Once again, it never occurred to us not to be open to life.

We hoped and prayed for a cure, but at no point did we refuse to accept God's will. Dallas was a gift. We cherished each day with him and treated him like a regular kid. For instance, I still disciplined him when it was necessary, but as with all my children, I always hugged him afterward.

I Wouldn't Change a Thing

When Connie became pregnant again, our doctor told us the baby could be tested and the pregnancy terminated if it was found to have CF or MD. I told the doctor, "We are going to have this baby and take care of it, no matter what."

Taunia was nine years old when our third child was born. "It's a boy," the doctor announced as he held up Matthew. My heart filled with love as I met my newest son. "Lord," I prayed, "it's all in your hands."

Matthew started out looking healthy. He didn't have CF. At least he will be spared that, we thought, realizing the grim prognosis we had been given regarding any boy babies. Matthew started walking at an early age. Then he started running. *What's going on here?* we wondered.

Only later did doctors determine that the muscular dystrophy must have been a one-time thing with Dallas and might not be hereditary after all. Good thing we put our trust in God, not man!

Three years later, Katie joined our family. Katie tested positive for CF, but fifteen years after Dallas' diagnosis, treatments had improved and life expectancy is now into the forties.

Dallas grew into a happy, outgoing, regular kid, even though by the age of ten, his increased muscle weakness forced him into a wheelchair. He understood his situation, but he never complained. "I'd rather be walking, but this is the way it is," he said once. When he was around thirteen, Connie got a call from his teacher because he was chasing girls in his wheelchair. The girls were flirting with him and he'd chase after them. "Good for him," I said. "He's just having fun and being a teenager."

We did our best to give Dallas a normal life. We often loaded his wheelchair into the back of the van and headed out to basketball games and other activities. Still, it would have been too hard for Dallas to sit out in the cold at a football game. We could never leave him alone at home. Ultimately, though, this brought our family closer together. The younger children adored their big brother and spent hours going for walks with him, playing, joking, and just talking with him.

We sometimes talked about dying. "Are you afraid of dying?" I asked him several times. He never was, except after an episode of choking. He had told me he did not ever want to die that way. "Then pray and ask God," I told him. Dallas never had a choking episode again.

"Dying is just part of living," Dallas would say. "You never know," he once stated, "you could go before I do."

"You're right," I agreed. "But however it happens, we will all be together again eventually," I explained. "And in heaven, with God, we will always be happy."

In a way, I saw it as a blessing that we wouldn't have to experience an unexpected death. Even the younger kids knew Dallas would not be with us long. Without the faith that we had, it would have been next to impossible to have these conversations. With faith however, life and death go together.

By the time Dallas was thirteen, he needed help lifting his books and going to the bathroom. This period of his life was often difficult. Kids his age were in sports and spending time with their friends. Dallas returned home after school, did physical therapy with Connie, and then lay on the couch until dinner. Towards the end, friends often came by to play games with him. While his CF had been kept under control, the MD was quickly taking him away from us.

Even though Dallas accepted his condition, he wanted as many years and days as he could have. Towards the end, he requested a wish from the Make-a-Wish Foundation, which was granted to him. He wanted to meet Magic Johnson, basketball player for the Los Angeles Lakers. Our whole family flew out to LA and visited Disneyland. Dallas, Matthew, and I were invited to sit in on a Lakers' practice and later meet with Magic. He came and sat with us and asked Dallas a few questions. Dallas was a little shy, but it was a wonderful experience. Dallas is the reason our whole family, including his nephews and nieces, are all Los Angeles Lakers fans.

One weekend, Connie and I knew the end was close. The doctor came by on Sunday morning and confirmed that it would not be long. Dallas's breathing was getting more labored. On Sunday afternoon, the other kids joined their grandparents for a church supper while Dallas and I watched the Minnesota Vikings play the Chicago Bears on TV. I was cheering for the Vikings and Dallas was rooting for the Bears. Connie kept busy nearby in the kitchen. Suddenly, I looked over at Dallas and saw that he could not breathe. I went over and held him in my arms. "Don't be scared," I told him, keeping my voice calm. "Just ask Jesus to take you home," I said. "Don't fight it. Don't hold back."

Connie came over and sat next to Dallas. Our eyes met. We were scared but neither of us wanted our son to suffer anymore. "Jesus, take him and take care of him," Connie cried. Then he slipped away in my arms. I was still holding him, but suddenly he was no longer there. He was with Jesus.

Dallas passed away on September 17, 1989, before the game ended. We wrapped him in a blanket, held him, and cried. Connie called a priest, who came to give him the sacrament of Last Rites but he was already gone. The TV was still on, and we realized the Bears had won. "Oh, you stinker," I laughed through my tears. "You're in heaven now, and your team won."

When the other children came home and discovered Dallas was gone, they all grieved differently. Matthew said, "He is in heaven now. We should be happy for him, not sad for ourselves." Connie and I were happy that Dallas was no longer suffering, but it was hard to say good-bye to our courageous, firstborn son.

Dallas would be thirty-nine if here were still alive. His illness never diminished the blessing he was in our lives. Had we not said yes to life after Dallas, our ten grandchildren would not be here. Our other three children are all married and have become parents themselves

Dallas brought us much love, and our family is closer because of him. I can honestly say that I would not have changed a thing. God takes care of us!

MY SUMMER VACATION

Sherry Antonetti

THIS PAST SUMMER, we packed up everyone for a road trip to Texas to participate in my brother's wedding. Driving over 3,000 miles in a twelve-passenger van may not seem like an idyllic experience, but in the glow of retrospect, it was an awesome journey! Since all my kids had to do a "What I Did on My Summer Vacation" report, it's only fair that I do one, too.

Every time I thought about packing for this jaunt, I got a headache and looked for something else to do. I tried making lists. Eventually, I recognized that this was not something I could just throw together. Since the whole thing felt like Trip Impossible, I imitated my favorite chef from *Restaurant Impossible* and got out my whiteboard to make a generic list of what we needed. Looking at it, I finally admitted how overwhelmed I felt. My kids looked at me as if I was crazy. "We can do it—that's easy!" Then they went to work, looking through the laundry to assemble their outfits. They didn't get through everything, but their enthusiasm was infectious, and we were able to get almost completely organized before a freak hurricane knocked out the power.

With the whole house plunged into darkness, the only sensible thing to do was send all helpers under the age of eleven to bed. The rest of us finished packing by flashlight. Why were the flashlights handy? Because the kids had been foraging through their school emergency kits. At one point they had turned off the lights for a light battle that turned into a heavy fight. I had taken away the instruments of illumination/destruction, and now they were easily accessible. Over the radio we heard how bad things actually were. I was just grateful we got out of town with only one night of pseudo-camping indoors.

The hotel we stayed at had a great free buffet breakfast and dinner. We lined up. We took over three tables. I looked at my children, who were delighted beyond reason by the seemingly endless bounty of waffles and chocolate milk, and I felt relief. They were civilized. The manager wasn't calling for my head. It wasn't my kids that pushed every button in the elevator (though I admit, if they'd made it to the panel first, it might have been).

Even more surprising was the way my children responded to the amenities of the trip itself. The television was not as captivating as the turtles we could see from the bird's eye view of our window. Taking six swimmers to the pool for an evening swim and watching my twelve-year-old do cannon balls with his new best friend was a delight. Why had I thought my kids would not be delighted by beauty (the ocean) or bored by travel? Why did the pleasure of their company, even in cramped quarters, surprise me? Because I had bought into the myth that taking a trip with ten children was impossible simply because I hadn't done it before. I'd succumbed to having a smaller and smaller world to manage rather than risk getting out there and living. Because I was out of my comfort zone, I almost shortchanged my kids—and our lives as a result. I knew God gives us the grace necessary for any task he has called us to do, but I'd allowed the day-to-day routine to grind my heart into forgetfulness.

My one regret from the whole trip was the wedding reception. We had babysitters for some of our younger children, and as a result they didn't get to see the cake or the dancing. They know from their siblings that they missed a party. By hindsight, if there is a chance for joy, dance, and celebration, even though it seems easier not to, the next time I will allow my children to be a part of it, at least for a while. They may be tired, they may go back to sleep, but then, at least, it was their decision; you didn't keep them from something wonderful.

My husband sagely planned an extra day on our return trip for a day at the ocean. You would think the road, hotels, celebrations, and family would have been sufficient, but he knew we would need a bit of quiet on our journey. The ocean and the sand and the slowness of that day would contrast with a return to "real life."

Ten kids, 3,085 miles, a twelve-passenger van, a hurricane,

a wedding, and a feast of memories created a lasting impression of family life in the hearts and minds of our children: crowded, messy, chaotic, filling, crazy, sometimes gross, fun, loud, quiet, joyous, luminous, glorious, and real.

There never was a question of whether we would make this trip, but it did seem impossible until we simply did it. To me, that's how God's plans often work. We would find our day-to-day lives much easier if we stopped competing with God's will and just lived. So what did I learn this summer? Never forget: It is no sacrifice to be surrounded by those that love us, and with God, all things are possible, even if not entirely easy.

FOR HEAVEN SNAKES!

Patti Maguire Armstrong

DURING OUR FIRST year living in the country, Mark and I embraced the great outdoors and everything that came with it. I always loved nature and adventure, but I was to learn that I had limits.

It was typical to find the boys outside building forts, catching critters and insects to keep in various containers, and even building an Indian village and trading post. We hatched chicks—and learned firsthand why it's not a good idea to help a chick escape an egg he has been unable to get out of himself for three days. (You don't want to know the rest of the story.)

When my husband Mark heard of a rattlesnake roundup in a nearby town, we thought it would be great fun for the boys to attend (and give the frogs a break.) I stayed home with our new baby and the toddler, but when they returned, I thoroughly enjoyed their enthusiastic descriptions of how the snakes were caught, decapitated, skinned, and then fried and served up for eating. The boys thought it was very cool to be able to say they had eaten rattlesnake.

The event left such a big impression on my kids that the following Monday they were still talking about it, particularly our two little nature boys: Luke and Tyler.

"Mom, I watched how they skinned the snakes, and I know I can do it," Luke reported.

"I do, too," Tyler chimed in.

"That's nice," I chuckled. "If we ever run out of food, we can eat snake."

We mothers must take care when we use sarcasm with our children lest they misunderstand. My own boys took my remark as permission. At the very least, they figured I didn't tell them *not* to skin snakes.

After our lessons were over and chores completed that day, I took advantage of a little quiet time to do some writing while the girls napped and the boys played outside. "Mom, we did it!" I heard a cry from the distance. Seconds later, Luke and Tyler appeared before me, proudly holding up their trophies. One boy held up an eight-inch snakeskin and the other held up some white, slimy looking meat. (Rest assured—it was a garter snake, not a rattler.)

But the big surprise was yet to come.

"Will you cook it for us now?" Tyler asked. Both boys stood wide-eyed, waiting for my answer.

"Cook it?" I asked incredulously.

"Yes," explained Luke. "You just need to bread it and fry it like they did with the rattlesnakes."

I knew that the boy's adventure would not be complete if they could not say they ate the snake. So, like any good homeschooling mother would do, I breaded the slimy meat and cooked it up until it looked like a big, fat onion ring. The boys were more than satisfied, and I considered it a good memory for them.

But I was wrong. Luke and Tyler had only just begun. Luke read books about curing snakeskins with salt. Soon he had quite a collection. (Sixteen years later we still have some of those skins.) And each time, we either cooked the meat or he wrapped it up to put it in the freezer for later. In case you are wondering, I never tasted the snake myself. The boys said it tasted like chicken, but I doubt it. They never really ate much of it. I suppose the bones got in the way, since they had no idea how to filet the thing.

Our snake adventures finally came to an abrupt halt one day when Luke, Tyler, and a neighbor boy caught the big daddy of them all. It was summer by then and windows were open, so I think everyone from miles around must have heard their loud shouts and excited screams. I ran outside to see what the commotion was about. The boys had caught a four-foot bull snake. No big game hunter could have been more excited. The neighbor boy's grandmother looked out her window from the hill above our house, laughing and waving. She was a kindred spirit, relishing the joy of watching three young boys embracing the country life.

The boys quickly skinned the snake, marveling at the large skin they had to cure now. But when they brought four-feet of slime into my kitchen to cook, I protested. "You don't really want to eat that, do you?" I questioned.

All three boys looked at me with surprise. Of course they wanted to eat it. This had been a big hunt, and they were ready for the big feast.

I looked at the meat. Chicken it wasn't. "Okay," I relented. "I'm going to cook this up, for one reason—because I love you. But this is going to be the last time. I'm not cooking anymore snake after this."

The boys agreed readily. I breaded the meat and put it into a big frying pan. It stiffened into a circle, looking like an onion ring on steroids. I served it up onto a big plate. The thick, stiff meat did not readily lend itself to cutting. Each boy took a bite and expressed pleasure. I have no doubt that it could have tasted like dirt and they would have responded the same. It was the idea of what they had accomplished that they loved, not the flavor of the serpent. After a few nibbles, each boy declared himself full and went onto the next adventure.

I kept my vow not to cook up another snake. Luke and Tyler, however, remember their snake-hunting adventures with relish. Although we eventually moved into town, certain children of mine still love to catch snakes at a park we frequent near the Missouri River. (I've refused to let them bring any home.)

I'm thinking of taking the younger kids to the rattlesnake roundup this year—I would like to see the event myself. However, there will be limits this time around. I often ask God to help me to stay as enthusiastic with the younger kids as I was with the older ones, but I'm asking for a waiver from heaven when it comes to snakes!

NOT WHAT WE PLANNED

Leon Suprenent

"DADDY, I'M PREGNANT."

My unmarried daughter's announcement last February forever changed our family. No longer could "unplanned pregnancies" or "single mothers" be spoken of in abstract terms, as things that only happen in other families. This was a flesh-and-blood reality that challenged us to renew our commitment to Christ and to our beloved firstborn daughter.

The early weeks of 2006 had some remarkable twists. On New Year's Day, hours before heading to Boston for my annual Ignatian retreat, my wife Maureen gave me the surprising yet wonderful news that she was pregnant. In February we learned that she was carrying twins, but our joy turned to sadness as one died in utero, followed by the other. While Maureen was still recovering from her seventh and eighth miscarriages, we learned that we were to become grandparents for the first time. Over the course of the next several months, we had our ups and downs, but we've come to see God's providential love for our family in a more profound way.

Like all Catholic parents, we've tried to provide all of our children with a solid formation in the Christian faith. While parents might disagree on the exact amount of "sheltering" that needs to take place, clearly during a child's formative years it's crucial to maintain some control over his or her environment and activities. But when our children become adults, we can't exercise the same type of control. We desire good things for our adult children, but we can't make decisions for them.

Maureen jokingly says, "I hate free will" when our children make bad decisions. If it were only up to us, our children would always choose Christ and his Church, and they would always choose that which is morally good. Yet they are all on their own journey to God, and we have to trust that the Lord will lead them to repentance and conversion in his time.

In this particular situation, we obviously could not undo the sins and bad choices our daughter had already made as an adult. Even more importantly, going forward we could not "control" the outcome, despite my conviction that "Father knows best" how to handle the situation. Maureen and I had to learn that what was needed was not control and coercion, but love, support, and wise guidance. Our daughter had to make her own difficult decisions, and that was scary.

In the weeks following this "bombshell," my daughter was inclined to place her child in an adoptive home. There is substantial irony in this, as Maureen and I have had several experiences of being adoptive parents. I affirmed my daughter's inclination to go the adoption route. The totality of her circumstances, not to mention the absence of a father, seemed to point clearly in that direction. At her request, I began looking for a couple that might be open to an independent adoption.

As a matter of principle, I knew that adoption would be a good, loving decision. At the same time, what grandparent does not want to be part of their grandchild's life? I have frequently called upon grandparents in that situation to be generous in supporting adoption, not placing undue pressure on the mother to keep their grandchild. The shoe was now on the other foot, so now it was my turn to walk the talk. I have learned to have more compassion and understanding for grandparents who don't want to "lose" their grandchildren.

As it turned out, however, our daughter really wanted to keep the child and be a full-time mother. She just couldn't see how it could all play out, given her difficult circumstances. I continued to encourage adoption and lovingly set forth the harsh realities of single motherhood. Even more, we encouraged her to grow in faith and responsibility. Over time, it became increasingly clear that her heart was set on keeping the child. We did our best to change gears and support this decision once it was firmly made. We invited her to move home rent-free so that she could be a full-time nursing mom. She accepted.

This required quite an adjustment for everybody. After being on her own for several years, our twenty-six-year-old had to deal not only with meddling parents and an elderly grandmother but also with five younger siblings ranging in age from fourteen to less than two. For our part, we had to get used to having an adult child in our midst, learning to balance our parental concern with the desire to give her appropriate freedom and space.

Slowly but surely, our daughter blended back into our household. She grew accustomed to the rhythm of our daily life, from our more conventional hours to prayer time, family meals, and our busy homeschool day. She has become, in some ways, more a part of our family than ever before. I'm very proud of her.

As our daughter's pregnancy became more obvious to all, I was so grateful for the love and compassion showed us by the families in our parish and community. I don't recall hearing any judgmental or condemning remarks. For myself, I remember a priest once saying that God's love, when focused on us sinners, shows itself as mercy. I wanted my daughter to come to a profound experience of God the Father's love for us. As a human father, I thought it was absolutely necessary to communicate to my daughter God's fatherly love and mercy. It surely wasn't the only thing, but it was the most important and Godlike thing.

Similarly, I've always wanted my family to see the Church as the family of God, our true and lasting home. Even though we might stray, the Good Shepherd goes looking for us, and there's great rejoicing in heaven when he finds us and brings us back into the fold. If my family would truly be a "domestic Church" or as Bl. John Paul II called it, a "sanctuary of life," I felt it was imperative to extend an arm of assistance, welcome, and unconditional love to my daughter in her time of need.

As our entire family eagerly awaited the newest Suprenant,

there was a subtle yet real strengthening of family relationships. Maureen became our daughter's labor coach and helped her get ready for childbirth and beyond. Finally, on June 13, the feast of St. Anthony, little Alexandra ("Alex") Marina Terese Suprenant was born. It didn't take much for this beautiful little child of God to steal her grandpa's heart.

Our daughter and baby Alex are a gift to the entire family. They share a room with my daughter Mary Kate, who loves being their "roommate." Alex has two doting uncles (Samuel, age five, and Raymond, age two) who consider themselves her bodyguards. Meanwhile, our daughter continues to grow and mature as a full-time mother. She has been a big help to her ailing grandmother, and she has become an indispensable part of our homeschooling operation as Samuel's kindergarten teacher this year. But beyond all that, her face looks happier than it has for many years.

My prayer is that my daughter and granddaughter will continue to live with us until the day, God willing, that our Lord calls her to the sacrament of marriage.

Of course, all of that is her decision, not mine.

THE TRICK TO BECOMING A SAINT

Theresa Kloska Thomas

I ADMIT, IT was a dirty trick. As I walked into the playroom with an armful of towels and other clean clothes, I enthusiastically asked three of my little girls, ages eight, six and three, "Who wants to be a saint?"

"I do!" they all shouted, before they saw my unfolded linens. By then they were trapped. Their little faces fell when they saw what I had in store—scrunched up towels, underwear, and socks. "No fair, Mommy," whined Grace, the six-year-old. "You said we get to be saints!" "You *do*," I explained, as I dumped my armload at their feet. "Becoming a saint, like St. Thérèsè said, is doing little things with great love. By offering up your time and helping when you don't want to, you have the opportunity to do something saintly. Now, let's fold!"

Lucky for me, they bought it and scrambled for the pieces of laundry, getting right to work. After awhile, though, the novelty wore off. A couple of the girls meandered to another room, undoubtedly looking for something more "fun." I pulled them back a couple times to finish the laundry task, and sat down with them to make it a little more endurable. When the last sock was matched and the stacks stood tall, I hugged them and told them how proud I was of them. "Look what a fine job you did," I praised.

Okay, I was sneaky, but God is sneaky too, I thought. Drawn in by great aspirations of being his saints, we enthusiastically pray, "I want to be a saint. Show me how!" and then we become frustrated when he sends a million little discomforts our way in our daily lives, not realizing that these are the hills he sets before us to climb to build up our strength and purify our wills. In doing what is necessary but not what we want, we can mortify ourselves and become holy. Jesus said, "If a man wishes to come after Me, he must deny his very self, take up his cross, and follow in My steps" (Mk 8:34). That means that every day, from breakfast through bedtime, no matter what our vocations, we have "yeses" to say. Washing dishes can be a means to sanctification. Reaching out to others can make us holy. Getting up early to go to work can help us on our path to heaven. Listening intently to our child when our minds want to rush into other thoughts can help us become saints.

Father Paul O'Sullivan, OP, who wrote the classic book, *An Easy Way to Become a Saint,* suggested that any ordinary Catholic can become a great saint without doing anything extraordinary. Just by living out one's vocation to the best of one's ability, and utilizing the opportunities that unfold each day, one can become holy and attain heaven.

A perfect example of this ordinary sanctity would be dear Mrs. Corey, a retired second-grade teacher and a member of our parish, who brought sunshine to everyone she met. I was amazed and humbled the day she stopped me after church and offered to come to my home and read to my children (at that time we had seven). Who was this person? Did she have nothing better to do? Why would she want to come to my home and read to my offspring? I'm so glad I said yes. The calming lilt of her voice mesmerized my children. Did I ever speak that way to them? I resolved then and there that I would from now on. She demonstrated something small done with great love.

Three months later it was Christmastime, and Mrs. Corey again stopped me after Mass. "Here is a bit of homemade cookie dough," she said, pushing a bowl of the sweet-smelling dough into my hands. "With so many children I'm sure you won't have time to make cookies from scratch this year." How did she know? I accepted with gratitude another little thing done with great love.

God invites all of us to become saints, and we may heartily reply "yes" before we know what we're in for. But we don't have to be afraid that he'll ask too much. Ordinary tasks done with extraordinary love will do the trick—simple, mundane, non-spectacular tasks, like reaching out to others, doing our daily duties well, going to work, and yes, simply helping to fold a pile of laundry.

YOU OWE ME TWO

Elizabeth Matthews

"OKAY, THAT'S IT," I said, as I dropped off bags of my maternity clothes to be taken to a home for unwed mothers. I was trying to cheer myself up about moving into a new phase of my life. Getting back in the car, I turned to check car seats before moving on. *You look so much like Sean,* I thought as I gazed at my little boy, Connor, who was now four years old. It had been nineteen years since my first child, Sean, was born, and now Connor was to be my last.

Connor was an answer to prayer. Five years earlier, from a medical standpoint, it looked like I would not be having any more children. God had blessed my husband, Mark, and me with nine beautiful children, and yet I continued to ask God to bless us with just one more. Sean had left a few years earlier to attend an apostolic school. It was hard to let him go, and yet after much prayer we felt it was God's will for him. When Connor was born, God had given me a little boy that would always remind me of Sean.

When Connor was two, I was pregnant once again with our eleventh child, Joseph Michael. God took him to heaven, however, long before he was big enough to hold in my arms. Two more years went by, and I was sure my time of having children was over, yet I continued to pray. Fully aware that God owed me nothing, I said, "You know God, now you owe me two. Twins would be beautiful." My daughter, Laura, had left home to prepare for life as a lay missionary, and my son, Brendan, feeling called to the priesthood, had followed his brother into the minor seminary school. I figured that, if God gave me Connor when Sean left, he was two babies behind with Laura and Brendan gone.

One day I asked my doctor, "What are the chances of me having twins?" She said that my chance of giving birth to twins was greater at my age because I could ovulate twice in one month. It was a glimmer of hope, but the possibility still seemed too far out of reach. Having left the last traces of maternity with my friend, Judy, in two very large black trash bags, I headed home.

Sixty-eight hours later my head started to explode with the familiar pain of a migraine. Just to be sure before taking my medication, I took a pregnancy test. I knew I could only be a little over three weeks, but I wanted to be sure. My hand started to shake, and tears of joy filled my eyes as the second pink line became darker and darker. God was blessing us with one more child, or so I thought.

Soon, I started experiencing unusual sharp pain, and my HCG blood levels were checked to make sure the pregnancy was not ectopic. In less then forty-eight hours, the levels had not doubled like they are supposed to—they had tripled. The doctor said, "I think it's twins." A short while later this was confirmed with an ultrasound. To my surprise, though, it was not the way my doctor had expected it might happen. I was not pregnant with fraternal twins from having ovulated twice in one month. There on the screen we could see one sack and two heartbeats. They were identical twins from one egg that had split. There is no scientific explanation for why it happens. It's another beautiful miracle from God.

Needless to say, I was in shock, but nothing like my husband, Mark. He knew how much I wanted and prayed for another child, but he didn't know I was secretly praying for twins. Mark has always been open to any new life God wanted to bless us with. Over the years he has seen how God has always provided, and yet the concern for two more little ones was heavy on his heart. This was compounded with fear for my health—he knew I did not handle pregnancy well and would likely be on bed rest for many months with complications.

My concerns were different. Within a short period of time the shock, joy, gratitude, and awe that filled my heart became overshadowed with worry and anguish. It wasn't from all the complications I read about on the Internet. I knew the babies were in God's hands, his precious gift to me. What filled me with fear was the kind words from well-meaning friends like, "You are such a good mother that God decided to give you two more," or "Obviously, God knew you deserve them." I knew that what they said could not be further from the truth. I knew my sinfulness, and I also knew that I did not deserve these precious little ones.

In my mind I could see only one possible solution. God would realize that I was not worthy of such a gift, and he would take them back to himself just like my little Joseph. In other words, God just needed to realize he had made a mistake. I started to plead with him. *I will try to do better; just let me keep them.* Then while pouring my fear out to God in prayer, I heard this in my heart, "You are right. You don't deserve them. You don't deserve any of your children. They are pure gifts of my love from all time according to my will." I was overcome with joy. The fear was lifted. Now I knew that the lives of my babies did not depend on my holiness, but on the will of God.

Over time I came to realize that God had never even taken Sean, Laura, or Brendan away. Physically we are apart, but when we let them go God gave them back to Mark and me in a spiritual way that is far more beautiful than we could have ever imagined.

As I write these words, two identical little boys, Johnny and Tommy, are taking my kitchen apart, and I couldn't be happier. They are identical to most of the world, but I think Johnny resembles Laura, and Tommy looks very much like Brendan. But, that's just me. As I watch them toddle about, in my heart I hear the words, "You owe me two." I answer with great joy, "Yes, Lord, I do. These little ones are yours. Thank you."

FROM RICHES TO RAGS

Mary Stutzman

AS A RECENT college graduate with a computer science degree, I started my job search. I agonized over having to accept a job that would move my fiancé and me across the country. Then, "out of the blue," a wonderful job opportunity opened up in my hometown. It was a large, international organization in an enviable work environment. I would make almost double what I expected coming right out of college. Of course, I took it.

Working in the corporate world as a computer analyst in the mid-1980s was exciting. I wore nice suits and worked with smart, interesting people all day. My husband and I were soon able to buy our first home and a bright red Camaro. We were living "the good life."

Our first two children were born eighteen months apart, and the demands of home and work began to wear on me. After five years in the corporate world, I started to question my priorities. Work was increasingly demanding, and I felt the maternal pull towards my little ones at home. I had a good babysitter, but I felt that she got the best part of my children's day. When their little arms wrapped around me at night, I began to think that working wasn't all it was cracked up to be.

One day, during a staff meeting, my boss imposed sixteen hours of mandatory overtime on my colleagues and me. I was still nursing my eight-month-old son, expressing milk throughout the day. "Will I be able to go home at the end of the day to eat dinner with my family and nurse my baby?" I asked. I was told no. Someone would need to bring the baby to me if I wanted to nurse him. I envisioned the scene: A brief rendezvous with my little family, hastily nursing my baby and kissing his sweet little head good-bye, and then saying good night to my husband and toddler daughter, I would return to the office for the remainder of the evening. There was no choice for me—I had to find a way out of this job that had once seemed so wonderful.

My husband came home from work that night to find me sitting on the floor of the family room, crying. Bills sprawled out all over the floor as I feverishly punched numbers into a calculator, trying to figure out a way to manage on his entry-level engineer's pay of $7.00 an hour. It was useless. There seemed no way for me to quit my job and for him to be the sole support of our family of four. I prayed. "Show me a way out, Lord!" I begged. "You understand how I want to be with my children. You know they need me. Show me a way!"

A few days later, a family friend called to ask if I wanted to do some part-time computer programming at home. It was an answer to my prayer! I quit my corporate job and never looked back.

I said good-bye to my business suits, nylons, and high-heels and hello to comfortable blue jeans, tennis shoes, and t-shirts (complete with spit-up stains on the shoulders and leaky milk spots on the front). The part-time work at home lasted for three years, and during this time baby number three came along and my husband's job began to generate an income on which we could live. We clipped coupons, shopped clearance racks, rummaged through garage sales, and drove used cars. Then came babies four, five, and six. Things got financially tighter. I couldn't be happier.

This is my life now, and I don't regret the choice I made to stay home and raise our children. Of course, we hear the occasional, "We'd probably be able to (fill in the blank) if Mom was still working"—"have a swimming pool," "drive a sports car," "wear designer shoes," "go out to dinner," etc. I don't mind, though. I've learned that the riches in this life aren't shiny red Camaros and corporate careers. The riches that matter are those we can't buy: a fruitful marriage, beautiful children, and a solid faith in God that he will direct us to the riches of heaven. Yes, my life is a success. Thank God for his grace to go from "riches to rags."

MOVING IN THE SPIRIT

Sue Elvis

IT WAS TIME to move—again.

My husband Andy and I lived on a fish farm in a tumble-down weatherboard cottage, surrounded by 100 acres of Australian bush. Each evening, with our five young children skipping at our heels, we wandered from dam to dam, feeding the fish. Startled kangaroos sometimes hopped out from under the trees, colorful birds swooped noisily overhead, and our cattle dog barked as black snakes slithered into the undergrowth at our approach. It was a quiet, peaceful life. We looked ahead and imagined our unborn baby joining our tribe and we were happy.

But the farm was not ours, and we heard it was going to be sold. Our quiet life became hectic as we searched for rental houses and started packing boxes. Although we were very busy, there was one appointment I had to make time for: a routine pregnancy ultrasound.

I drove into town for the appointment late one afternoon. I was about to see my son for the first time, but my mind was filled with houses and application forms, packing boxes and removal trucks. On the return journey, unchecked tears rolled down my face. It had not turned out to be a routine ultrasound after all. I was the mother of an unborn baby who had "an abnormality incompatible with life." Our son was almost certain to die after birth. Instead of thinking about houses, I wanted to be alone with my grief and fear, but that was impossible.

After several weeks of house-hunting, we still had not found a home. I had viewed properties, filled in applications forms, and sat by the phone waiting for answers with no result. *Could the number of children account for the fact that none of our applications had been approved?* I wondered. Andy's days were consumed with work and long hours of travel, so it was up to me to search.

I was very familiar with the house-hunting routine. We had regularly moved from one rental property to another as our family grew in size and number. The more children we had, the less attractive our family appeared to landlords, or so it seemed. Sometimes I felt rather envious of all my home-owning friends. No one ever questioned how many children they could have living in their homes. No one ever said, "Another baby? How will you ever find a home for so many children?" They could stay in one place and enjoy their growing families, while we had to continually keep moving.

One day, the phone rang. I heaved my pregnant body reluctantly off the bed where I had been resting. The real estate agent wanted to know if I could come into town that afternoon and view several more rental properties. I was tired and sunk in grief, and although I said yes, I was convinced that all the effort would not be worth it. If we did find our dream home, would the landlord be willing to rent to us when he found out we had five children?

God had always looked after us, and I knew all we had to do was trust him. But sometimes I did not want to trust. I did not want to worry about what other people thought of the size of our family. But the reality was that we needed somewhere else to live, and that meant agreeing to view whatever houses were available. Driving to town, I imagined the conversation:

"How many children do you have?" asks the landlord.

"Five," I reply, hoping that sounds like his dream family instead of a large, noisy crowd. I stand tall, trying to hide my expanding stomach. Is it obvious that I am pregnant? Is he looking at me and thinking, "She means six, not five"? I see his glance and I say, "It might look like we will have six children, but we won't. Our baby won't need a home. He is going to die."

Of course, I only say such words in my imagination. They are far too shocking to say out loud. It doesn't matter if it is easier to find a home for five children rather than six. I want that sixth child with all my heart.

This move was different from the others. This time, we not only needed a home, we needed a refuge to wait for the birth of our child and then to recover from his death. Would one of the houses I was on my way to see be such a place?

I toured the first two houses and quickly realized they were unsuitable. With a heavy heart, I viewed the third house, not expecting much. But God had a huge surprise for me. The house was nestled behind a garden of tall, flowering shrubs. I walked up the path and through the front door and immediately thought, *This is perfect…if only…could we possibly have a chance of renting this?*

"What do you think?" asked the agent.

More importantly, what would the landlord think of us?

We had never lived in such a beautiful house before. It was huge and bright and clean, with a designer kitchen perfect for Andy who loves cooking, a garden just waiting for a swing set, pale-pink luxurious carpets, a park across the road, cupboards and more cupboards—everything a big family could ever need. I wanted to live there.

I was up front with the agent. "If we applied for this house, do you honestly think we'd have a chance? We have five children. How does the landlord feel about children?"

"I don't think there will be a problem. I'll phone him tonight and have an answer for you tomorrow morning."

For the next few hours, we all quivered with excitement. Had we found our refuge? The next morning we learned we had the house—somewhere to live and face the birth and probable death of our child.

We named our baby Thomas. He lived for a day. Then, we closed the door on the world and grieved. Together, we seven souls closed ranks within our beautiful, safe refuge chosen for us by God.

Eventually, light returned to our lives—and new life, too,

when we found out we were expecting another baby. We shared our exciting news, but some people were not so happy for us. "Do you think it's sensible to risk any more pregnancies?" Not only had we lost Thomas but also five other babies by miscarriage. Would this new precious soul also be with us for only a fleeting moment? We had no idea, but we trusted God to look after us.

This time all went well, and Sophie was born eighteen months after Thomas died. But when she was still a baby, we received a phone call from the real estate agent. "I'm very sorry," he began. "I wanted to tell you personally rather than in a letter, as you've been such good tenants. The landlord wants to move back into his house."

My oldest daughter Felicity cried at the news. I wanted to cry as well. I tried to sound positive. "God will find us another home. We love this house, but it's time to move on to new adventures." My voice was wobbly, but deep in my heart I knew my words were true.

Other people did not see it in the same light as we did, and some let us know. I went in tears to see our parish priest.

"Father, I've been told it's our own fault we don't have a home of our own. Should we have waited until we could have afforded to buy a home of our own before having children? Perhaps we shouldn't have had so many? Children need a secure home instead of being dragged from one rental property to another...or so we've been told. "

The priest reassured me. "You can try to seek security and stability through your own efforts. You can work hard and buy homes of your own and have money in the bank in order to obtain security, but such security is only an illusion."

I will never forget his next words: "Homes can disappear even if you own them. Circumstances can change overnight. True security comes only from trusting God. Your children are totally secure within your family."

So, once again, we went looking for a house, this time one for six children. I visited a real estate agent in town and told him exactly what we were looking for.

"You'll never find a house like that for the price you're willing to pay," he replied, shaking his head.

"But that's what we're paying for our current house," I said. He looked like he did not believe me. I thought about our dream home that had appeared just at the right moment. Why had the rent been so low? Why were we the only people who had viewed it? It was obvious: God had arranged that house just for us. He would help us again.

Eventually I heard about a cottage that sounded appropriate. The agent shrugged her shoulders when I asked about it. "Yes, it's cheap. It's not much of a house." The cottage was on the edge of town, surrounded by fields of cows and an overgrown garden. I waded through the long grass with Sophie in my arms, climbed carefully up the wobbly back steps and walked through the rickety porch door. Inside were threadbare carpets and damaged walls with peeling paint. I thought, *We could make a home here.* It was as if God whispered in my ear, "This will be your next home. I have chosen it for you."

But would the landlord approve of our six children? I turned to the agent, "It would make a great home. We have six children. Do you think that's a problem? They have lived in rental properties all their lives. They know how to take care of a house."

"Well, it's hardly a palace," the woman admitted. "They couldn't really do any more damage." She paused for a moment and I held my breath, and then she continued with a smile, "Yes, the house is meant for a family."

Soon we were moving into our new home. It was not a large cottage, but once we had unpacked our possessions, it felt like home. We were very happy there. We loved the peaceful, quiet location where the children could run and make lots of noise; the large garden with a row of shady pine trees and a gnarled old crab-apple tree perfect for climbing; and the view from the windows that looked out across the fields. We didn't even mind chasing the black-and-white cows back through the sagging wire fence.

One day we announced that another baby was on her way, and Felicity smiled and said, "Our home has elastic walls. There's always room for one more." And there was. No one minded being a bit more crowded when Gemma-Rose joined the family.

And then we were told that our cottage was going to be knocked down to make room for a new housing estate. Once again we were packing boxes, dismantling our home, and house-hunting. After nearly twenty-five years of renting homes, we knew the routine.

"St. Joseph will find us a new home," I said confidently.

"Why don't you ask St. Joseph for a home of our own?" Felicity asked.

A home of our own? Why had I never done this before? Was it an impossible request? I had always assumed that, because we were living on only one wage and had so many dependent children, no bank would consider giving us a mortgage. There was also the not-so-small problem of a deposit.

I changed my prayer: "St. Joseph, please pray for us. We'd really like a home of our own."

Not long after, we inherited some unexpected money. We nervously approached the bank. Would they consider approving our mortgage now that we had a deposit? To our great surprise, our application was approved. Instead of inquiring, "Do you have any houses to rent?" we announced, "We want to buy a house big enough for a large family." There was no longer any need to be nervous about our family size.

Twenty-five years after our wedding day, Andy insisted on carrying me over the threshold of our very own home. Our children trooped through the door after us with huge grins on their faces. We were moving into *our* house—no landlords, no restrictions. We could hammer as many picture hooks into the walls as we wanted. We could paint the walls any color we liked. God had decided it was time for us to become homeowners.

When Andy and I set out on our married life many years ago, we thought we had our future all mapped out. Somewhere along the way, we lost control of our lives and God took over. Life became an adventure. Thirteen homes; seven living children; eight children already with God; a lot of grief but also so much joy and love—and finally, a home of our own! Our adventure continues. Whatever happens, we know God will always look after us.

Almost at the end of the road, nestled between the gum trees, is a cream-colored brick house, half-hidden by flowering shrubs where fairy wrens and butterflies flit and flutter among the leaves. Inside the house, dozens of picture hooks have been pounded into the walls, and numerous images of the Madonna and Child look down upon the family who live there.

We whisper, "Thank you, St. Joseph!" And for now, we enjoy.

WHY WOMEN COOK

Theresa Kloska Thomas

SITO WAS MY late grandmother-in-law. No matter when my husband and I stopped by, Sito would provide a feast for us. She spent almost every day cooking and filling her freezer with nourishing delicious meals and treats, betting on the chance that someone would visit—if not this afternoon, then the next. When you'd spill your troubles to Sito, she'd say affectionately, "Awww, Dino, go get yourself a plate." And she would motion to the stove where a banquet that would feed an army sat hot and ready.

For generations, cooking food has been about more than just feeding one's body. It has always been a way to nourish a soul, a relationship, and to provide companionship and sustenance in a world that is sometimes cold. A hearty meal with family and friends, complete with hot bread and smooth, creamy butter, sometimes topped off with a bit of wine and finished with a cup of steaming coffee, is the way women nurture those they love, putting material form to their feelings. If they don't know what to do for someone, they cook. After the births of babies of their friends. For funeral dinners. At Christmastime—not only to celebrate the holiday of Christ's birth with decorated cookies and homemade candy, turkey with orange sauce, and cheesy potatoes, but to put tangible life and love into their devotion for their families. When there's nothing left to say, a woman can cook, and things somehow seem a little brighter. In lovingly preparing food, a woman hopes she is making a difference.

A woman will hover over a family member about to bite into a concoction that took all afternoon to create. She studies every eyebrow, every tilt of the head, in anticipation, hoping to see pleasure on her loved one's face. Seeing that will have made the effort worthwhile, and when she puts her floury, dusty apron away, she will be satisfied.

We live in the heart of Amish country, and I've been blessed to have some Amish ladies occasionally help me with my cleaning. Once, I heard the ladies talking about Cousin Nettie's wedding. Everyone in the community, young and old, pitched in to make food for the special day. The cooking began several days in advance, and was truly a social event in itself for the womenfolk. When Amish women want to shower their blessings on someone, they start at the stove.

While interviewing World War II veterans some years ago, one thing that impressed me was the fondness with which each man spoke about his first meal home after the war. I imagine those wives and mothers of men, now long gone, standing at the stove, praying and preparing. What else could they do?

Why Women Cook

Yesterday, my husband and I spent the afternoon in the kitchen together, making sfeeha (Lebanese meat pies), stuffed grape leaves, lentils with onions and rice, and Arabic bread—all recipes Sito shared with us before she died. It took us awhile to get in the groove of working together. Apparently, I was folding the sfeeha dough wrong, and he was definitely hogging the lemon juice. But once we found a rhythm, it was a very enjoyable endeavor. As the meat sizzled, cooking inside the oven, I felt pride in what my husband and I were creating—a meal yes, but more than that, a token of love for our family. You see, what precipitated the entire afternoon of cooking was the knowledge that it was the last day our college-aged sons would be home before going back to school. We wanted to prepare a meal for them that they would love.

Today, after receiving many hugs from their younger sisters and brother, the boys will return to the university, with a carload of their things and some grocery items. And in the back seat are some Tupperware containers of Lebanese food and some miniature apple pies, the fruits of yesterday's labor.

As I stand in the driveway, I wrestle with my feelings. I love these boys intensely. I want to see them follow their dreams and succeed. I am proud of them. I am happy. I am sad. I wish I could shield them from life's sorrows. I want them to know I'm here for them. For these reasons and a million more, I prepare food for them. And in doing so, I connect not only with my own family but with millions of women around the world. We cook simply because we love.

BLESSINGS WE ALMOST MISSED

Patti Maguire Armstrong

I WAS BORN a baby lover. I loved my baby dolls, I loved baby-sitting when I got older, and I loved taking care of my two little brothers. Growing up as the second oldest child in a family of eight, I often wished we had an even bigger family. So it was sadly ironic that I chose to limit our family's growth through unnatural means. It seemed that the desire God had planted in my heart to have children expired after having four of our own.

When our son Aaron was born, my heart overflowed. He was so cute and smart. I enjoyed every moment of motherhood. Luke, who came two years later, was gentle and cuddly. Two years later Tyler joined the family and kept us entertained with his early athletic prowess and happy personality. I loved my little boys with all my heart, but just how much love did a mother need? Weren't three little bundles of joy enough? Between the work required to be a parent and our modern society's standard of two kids per family, I decided three was definitely enough.

My husband, Mark, was not so sure, but he didn't want to pressure me. I decided to have surgery for a tubal ligation. Prior to surgery, during the pre-op exam, the doctor explained the failure rate was only one in 500. Those odds were unsettling. A failure could result in a tubal pregnancy, which could result in death. I canceled the next day.

The next plan was to go on birth control pills provided by my family physician, who was also my parish priest. Yes, you read that correctly. He was a priest who later received his bishop's permission to become a doctor. This doctor/priest was kind and much loved by his parishioners. I thought it would be great to have my doctor also as my priest. "It's not reasonable to expect couples to follow the pope's teaching on birth control," he told me.

I had interviewed him previously for a newspaper article, so I knew that birth control was an issue he preferred not to comment on publicly. Although I was an uninformed Catholic at the time, I did understand that birth control caused controversy within the Church. I simply was not clear on why, nor did I think it was necessary to agree with the Church on everything. And here was a priest, who was acting against the Church that he had promised to obey on the day of his ordination. Sadly, rather than setting us straight with Catholic teaching, he gave us the green light to ignore it.

I had problems with the birth control pills, so I stopped taking them. The following month I discovered I was pregnant. When Mark heard the news, he announced, "I've been praying for this!" It turned out the big sneak had been praying behind my back. Regardless, a die-hard baby lover like myself could not help but rejoice that we had another child growing within me.

Jacob was born on May 13, the anniversary date of Our Lady of Fatima's first appearance in Fatima, Portugal. It was also Mark's birthday and Mother's Day. Mark also had been born on Mother's Day thirty-three years earlier. Happy Birthday, Mark—from God.

During this time in our lives, we read about various Marian apparitions and were inspired for the first time to pray the Rosary. We stopped missing Sunday Mass and began learning more about our Faith. Still, we were not fully converted yet, particularly when it came to family planning. I insisted that Mark have a vasectomy, thinking that four pregnancies on my part were all I wanted to ever go through. Mark resisted at first, still wanting to be open to life, but finally relented.

Initially, I was oblivious that we had done anything wrong. But as I started making visits to the tabernacle, continued praying the Rosary, and desiring to do God's will, I grew in understanding. I realized that the Church, which Christ had founded to guide us until the end of time, had been given authority to teach on spiritual matters, including procreation, and that teaching has remained unchanged since apostolic time. I, on the other hand, had been given no such authority.

Mark and I had not turned to the wisdom and authority of the Church to make decisions in our lives. I shared these thoughts with Mark as it related to his vasectomy, but it seemed my understanding had come a little too late. He had been reluctant to go along with my idea to begin with, and he accused me of being like Eve. I agreed, but told him, "Remember, Adam was kicked out of the garden, too."

We prayed to God in contrition for not following Church teaching, and we told him that we desired to be open to whatever he wanted in our lives. We had heard stories of failed vasectomies, so in our mind, if God really wanted us to have more children, the vasectomy would fail.

One night I had a dream. I saw two babies: one blonde and one dark-haired. I felt an intense love for these babies, as if they were my own. At the end of the dream, I understood that these were babies God had planned for us, but because we had interfered with his plan, they would never be born. I woke up grieving. I knew the only solution was to convince Mark to have a reversal.

When Mark came home from work the next day, I approached him with the idea of a reversal. "No way!" he said. He declared the subject officially closed.

Now, it was my turn to pray behind Mark's back. "I want to do your will, God," I prayed, "but I am powerless to change Mark's mind. I'm putting everything in your hands." Then I just kept praying.

A couple months passed. One morning when we went out for breakfast after Mass, Mark casually wondered how much a vasectomy reversal would cost. "$10,000," I announced. Before

Mark had time to shoot my idea down, I called the doctor's office to get all the information.

"Well, I can't get off from work this month," Mark said, "but next month I could go in and get it done." I was shocked and thrilled. We did not have the money to pay for it, but we thought we could probably make payments.

"What changed your mind?" I asked. Mark's answer took my breath away.

"I had a dream last night," Mark said. "I saw two babies that God had planned for us." (I had never told anyone about my dream.)

"Mark, I had that same dream," I said. "That was the reason I wanted you to have a reversal." We just looked at each other as the immensity sunk in. God had made his will known to us.

Three months later we were expecting a baby. I had a strong feeling that it would be our first girl, and I thought God wanted us to name her Mary after the Blessed Mother who had intervened for us. We had never considered that name with our previous babies. I believed that if this inspiration was from God, he would let Mark know without me saying anything. I wrote on a slip of paper, "Yes, I think Mary would be a good name," and tucked it in my wallet. When Mark brought up the choice of a name to me, I planned to pull it out.

Our blonde-haired baby girl, Mary, was born on December

22, 1993. A few months before her birth, we inherited the exact amount of money needed to pay Mark's reversal surgery in full.

Dark-haired Teresa was born on my birthday, April 18, 1996. I thought we must be done at six children, now that we had the babies from our dream. However, Mark often said he thought ten children would be a good number. While praying about it, I recalled that when St. Maximilian Kolbe was young, he received a vision of Our Blessed Mother. She showed him two crowns of roses: a red crown representing martyrdom and a white one representing purity. She asked him which he would like to choose. He chose both. I wondered, just like St. Maximilian, could we volunteer to take on more than God asked? We prayed and remained open to life.

John was born on August 31, 1999, and Isaac was born on Mary's birthday, December 22, 2001. There could be no greater blessing for our family than our children. The younger ones help keep the older ones coming home to be a part of their sibling's lives. For instance, one year when Aaron and Luke were in their mid-twenties, they told me they had considered taking a trip to the tropics for Christmas. "But then we thought about John and Isaac," Aaron said, "and how they would feel if we didn't come home for Christmas. We decided we can take the trip later."

Even their friends have enjoyed the younger ones. One day, after Tyler had graduated from high school, a friend of his stopped by our house during a college break. "Tyler's not home right now," I said.

"Oh, I'm not here for Tyler," he said. "I came here to see John and Isaac." My two youngest came running up and jumped into his arms for a hug. He had no younger siblings at home.

Sometimes, I mentally take the youngest five children out of our family and imagine what life would be like had we stopped at three. People often say that you don't miss what you don't know, but I do know—I am so thankful that we did not miss out on our youngest children.

And as for Mark's opinion that ten children would be a good number for us, he did get his wish, but the rest of our blessings came to us from Kenya. We became parents to two boys whose parents had died of AIDS, but that's a whole other story.

Editors note: See page 1 for the rest of this story.

ABOUT THE AUTHORS

PATTI MAGUIRE ARMSTRONG *is an award-winning writer and speaker from Bismarck, North Dakota. She was managing editor and co-author of Ascension Press's Amazing Grace Series and has appeared on EWTN and Catholic TV as well as radio stations across the country.*

THERESA KLOSKA THOMAS *is a wife and full-time home-schooling mother from South Bend, Indiana. She is an award-winning author and family columnist for Today's Catholic News, a contributor to several Amazing Grace books, and has been a frequent guest on national and local Catholic radio.*

TOM MAHALA *is managing director for BNP Paribas in New York. He has been happily married to his wife Bonnie since 1991. They live in New Jersey with their boys and one daughter: Thomas, Kevin, Jack, Michael, Patrick, Luke, William, and Grace.*

KATE COATES *is a wife to Ryan, a student, and a mother of five fabulous kids. She is raising them some days with panache, others...not so much. Kate aspires to live well and be all God intends her to be. Find Kate at* http://katecoates.posterous.com.

CALVIN BADER *lives with his family on thirteen wooded acres. He works as a radio and TV engineer and Donna is a full-time homemaker.*

GAE ONIONS *is the mother of six boys and six girls. She and her husband, Stephen, live in Wagga Wagga, Australia. They love rural life and raising their children, and they look forward to owning their own self-sufficient farm soon. Gae blogs at Cherished Hearts at Home at this link:* cherishedheartsathome.blogspot. com.au.

DEEANN SMITH, MA, *is a conflict resolution specialist, trained in community-based mediation. A former news anchor from Dallas, she is the founder and host of the* "It's Up to Us!" *radio program, which features stories about Catholic women who live and lead with faith. She and her husband, David, have five children and live in Austin, Texas.*

KATHY CHARLEY *is the mother of twelve children. Prior to becoming a full-time mom, Kathy had a less glamorous career as a teacher of the hearing impaired at both the elementary and university levels. God's gift of motherhood has been her greatest reward.*

STACY TRASANCOS, PhD, *is a scientist turned homemaker. Chief editor at Ignitum Today and a senior editor at Catholic Lane, she is pursuing a MA in Theology at Holy Apostles College and Seminary. She writes about all that she is learning on her blog,* Accepting Abundance. *Stacy, her husband, and their seven opinionated children live in New York.*

FRANK RUSSO *has a BEE from Manhattan College and an MBA from Baruch. He is president of the American Family Association of New York. He has appeared on numerous TV news programs and talk shows, including* Larry King Live, Phil Donahue, *and* Geraldo *and has participated in many debates on college campuses. Frank has been married for forty-nine years. He and his wife have seven children and thirty-one grandchildren.*

JEFFERY GROSS *has been married to Connie for over forty years. They live in North Dakota and are the parents of four children (one in heaven) and eleven grandchildren. Jeff worked for Cenex for over thirty-seven years and has farmed for seven years. He treasures his time with family and friends.*

SHERRY ANTONETTI *is a Catholic writer, happily married and mother to ten beautiful children. You can read more at her blog,* http://www.sherryantonettiwrites.blogspot.com *or check out her first voyage into fiction when* The Book of Helen *is released (for e-books only), in May of 2013.*

LEON SUPRENANT *is the director of catechesis and program development for* www.mycatholicfaithdelivered.com, *an online Catholic learning center. He has written many books and articles on the Catholic faith. He resides with his family in the Archdiocese of Kansas City, Kansas.*

ELIZABETH MATTHEWS *is the author of* Precious Treasure, the Story of Patrick *and with her husband, Mark,* A Place for Me. *Elizabeth also has written previously for the Amazing Grace series.*

The Matthews are founders of Chelsea Shire Communications, a publishing and speaking apostolate. A "retired" nurse, she and her husband are the homeschooling parents of twelve children and reside in Indiana. For more information, please see Elizabeth's website, www.chelseashire.com.

MARY STUTZMAN *has been married to Scott, her high-school sweetheart, for almost thirty years and resides in their hometown of Elkhart, Indiana. Daughter Sarah and oldest son Greg both enjoy happy marriages. Son Adam is away at college, while Mary continues to homeschool her youngest three boys, Jacob, Matthew, and Philip. While being a grandma is her favorite pasttime, she also enjoys singing in the church choir, teaching CCD, reading, and sewing.*

SUE ELVIS *and her husband, Andy, have been married for twenty-nine years. They live with their eight children in the beautiful Southern Highlands, south of Sydney, Australia. Sue is involved in grief ministry and is the author of* Grief, Love, and Hope *and a children's book,* Angels of Abbey Creek, *which she hopes to soon publish. Visit her blog at* www.sueelviswrites.com.